NORMANDY

A GRAPHIC HISTORY OF D-DAY

THE ALLIED INVASION OF HITLER'S FORTRESS EUROPE

WRITTEN & ILLUSTRATED BY
WAYNE VANSANT

First published in 2012 by Zenith Press, an imprint of MBI Publishing Company,
400 First Avenue North, Suite 400, Minneapolis, MN 55401 USA

Zenith Press titles are also available at discounts in bulk quantity for industrial or
sales-promotional use. For details write to Special Sales Manager at MBI Publishing Company,
400 First Avenue North, Suite 400, Minneapolis, MN 55401 USA.

To find out more about our books, join us online at www.zenithpress.com.

ISBN: 978-0-7603-4392-0

Editor: Erik Gilg
Design Manager: James Kegley
Design: Wayne Vansant
Layout: Trevor Burks
Cover design: Wayne Vansant

Printed in China

CONTENTS

Allied and Axis Divisions, Normandy Campaign, Summer 1944

US Airborne Divisions
82nd Airborne "All American"
101st Airborne "Screaming Eagles"

US Infantry Divisions
1st Infantry "Big Red One"
2nd Infantry "Indian Head"
3rd Infantry "Rock of the Marne"
4th Infantry "Ivy"
5th Infantry "Red Diamond"
8th Infantry "Golden Arrow"
9th Infantry "Old Reliables"
28th Infantry "Keystone"
29th Infantry "Blue and Grey"
30th Infantry "Old Hickory"
35th Infantry "Santa Fe"
79th Infantry "Cross of Lorraine"
80th Infantry "Blue Ridge"
83rd Infantry "Thunderbolt"
90th Infantry "Tough Hombres"

US Armored Divisions
2nd Armored "Hell On Wheels"
3rd Armored "Spearhead"
4th Armored "Name Enough"
5th Armored "Victory"
6th Armored "Super Sixth"
7th Armored "Lucky Seventh"
2nd French Armored

British Airborne Divisions
6th Airborne "Red Devils"

British Infantry Divisions
3rd Infantry "Ironsides"
15th Infantry "Scottish"
43rd Infantry "Wessex"
49th Infantry "West Riding"
50th Infantry "Northumbrian"
51st Infantry "Highland"
53rd Infantry "Welsh"
59th Infantry "Straffordshire"

British Armoured Divisions
Guards Armoured
7th Armoured "Desert Rats"
11th Armoured "Black Bull"
79th Armoured (Experimental)

Canadian and Polish Divisions
1st Polish Armoured "Black Devils"
2nd Canadian Infantry
3rd Canadian Infantry
4th Canadian Armoured

German Infantry Divisions
77th Infantry
84th Infantry
85th Infantry
89th Infantry
243rd Infantry (Static)
265th Infantry
266th Infantry
271st Infantry
275th Infantry
276th Infantry
277th Infantry
319th Infantry (Static)
326th Infantry
331st Infantry
343rd Infantry
346th Infantry
352nd Infantry
353rd Infantry
363rd Infantry
709th Infantry (Static)
711th Infantry (Static)
716th Infantry (Static)

Luftwaffe Divisions
3rd Fallschirmjäger
5th Fallschirmjäger
17th Luftwaffe Field
91st Luftlande

German Panzer Divisions
Panzer Lehr
2nd Panzer
21st Panzer
116th Panzer
1st SS Panzer "Liebstandarte SS Adolf Hitler"
2nd SS Panzer "Das Reich"
9th SS Panzer "Hohenstaufen"
10th SS Panzer "Frundsberg"
12th SS Panzer "Hitlerjügend"
17th SS Panzergrenadier "Goetz von Berlichinger"

... GOODNIGHT THEN. SLEEP TO GATHER STRENGTH FOR THE
MORNING. FOR THE MORNING WILL COME. BRIGHTLY IT WILL
SHINE ON THE BRAVE AND TRUE, KINDLY UPON ALL WHO SUFFER
FOR THE CAUSE, GLORIOUS UPON THE TOMBS OF HEROES.
THUS WILL SHINE THE DAWN. VIVE LA FRANCE!

– WINSTON CHURCHILL,
IN A RADIO SPEECH TO
NAZI-OCCUPIED FRANCE,
OCTOBER, 1940

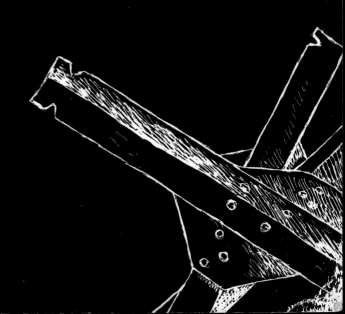

INTRODUCTION

THE THING THAT MOST PEOPLE NOTICE FIRST ABOUT THE REGION IS THE QUIET, PASTORAL SETTING. THE SLOW WATERS OF THE DOUVE AND VIRE RIVERS WHERE THE CATTLE COME RIGHT DOWN TO DRINK AND EAT THE BUTTERCUPS AND MALLOWS. THE WAGTAILS, KINGFISHERS, AND DRAGONFLIES DARTING AMONG THE HEDGEROWS. THE TALL CORNFIELDS IN THE SHADOW OF THE L'ABBAYE D'ARDENNE NEAR CAEN. IT IS A REGION THAT BOTH TIME AND HISTORY SEEMS TO HAVE PASSED BY.

HISTORY, HOWEVER, WOULD CAST ITS SHADOW ACROSS THIS REGION IN MANY STRANGE AND TERRIBLE WAYS. IT WAS IN THE TOWN OF FALAISE, IN 1027, THAT A YOUNG GIRL NAMED ARLETTE WOULD GIVE BIRTH TO THE ILLEGITIMATE SON OF ROBERT THE DEVIL, DUKE OF NORMANDY. DESPITE THE CIRCUMSTANCES OF HIS BIRTH, YOUNG WILLIAM WOULD EMBARK FOR THE INVASION OF BRITAIN, DESTINED TO MEET HAROLD OF ENGLAND ON THE FIELDS OF HASTINGS...

...IN THE SUMMER OF 1944, HISTORY WOULD AGAIN CAST ITS SHADOW ACROSS NORMANDY...

AND THE DEVIL WOULD RETURN TO FALAISE.

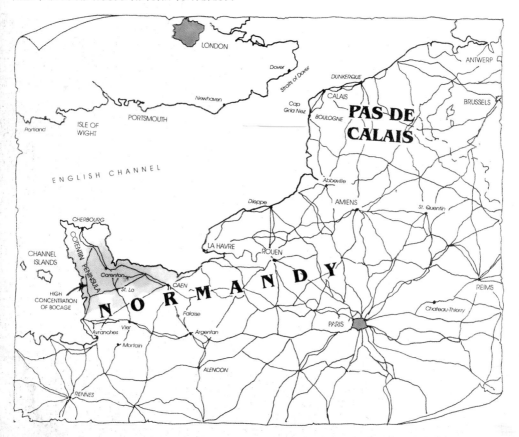

BY THE SPRING OF 1944, NAZI GERMANY WAS IN
RETREAT ON EVERY FRONT. AFTER MANY HUGE AND BLOODY
BATTLES ON THE RUSSIAN FRONT, THE SOVIET ARMY HAD
PUSHED THE GERMANS BACK TO THE POLISH BORDER. IN
ITALY, THE BRITISH AND AMERICANS HAD CAPTURED ROME.
ALLIED BOMBERS MADE RAIDS ON GERMAN INDUSTRY DAY
AND NIGHT.

NONETHELESS, ALLIED PLANNERS IN LONDON KNEW THAT IF
THEY WERE TO DEFEAT GERMANY, THEY HAD TO CROSS THE
ENGLISH CHANNEL AND INVADE THE EUROPEAN CONTINENT
ITSELF. NOW, AFTER 4 YEARS, THE "MORNING" THAT MR.
CHURCHILL HAD SPOKEN ABOUT WAS APPROACHING.

NORMANDY
CHAPTER ONE
SECOND FRONT NOW!

THE FIRST AMERICAN INFANTRYMEN ARRIVED IN GREAT BRITAIN IN JANUARY, 1942. IT WAS LESS THAN 2 MONTHS SINCE THE JAPANESE HAD BOMBED PEARL HARBOR, BRINGING THE UNITED STATES INTO THE SECOND WORLD WAR. MILLIONS MORE AMERICANS WOULD FOLLOW. AIRMEN TO FLY THE PLANES BOMBING GERMAN WAR INDUSTRY. SEAMEN TO MAN THE SHIPS BRINGING SUPPLIES ACROSS THE ATLANTIC AND FIGHT THE U-BOAT MENACE. AND MANY, MANY MORE SOLDIERS TO HELP ENGLAND IN NORTH AFRICA AND TO FIGHT THE FUTURE ITALIAN CAMPAIGN.

EVERYONE, HOWEVER, KNEW THE MAIN REASON THAT ALL THESE AMERICANS HAD COME TO ENGLAND.

SOONER OR LATER, THE COMBINED ALLIED POWERS (THE UNITED STATES, GREAT BRITAIN, CANADA, AND THE FREE FRENCH FORCES) WOULD HAVE TO CROSS THE ENGLISH CHANNEL AND ASSAULT THE "ATLANTIC WALL." THE WORLD HAD COME TO KNOW IT AS HITLER'S "FORTRESS EUROPE," WHICH STRETCHED FROM THE SPANISH BORDER TO SCANDINAVIA.

THERE HAD BEEN LONG-TERM PRESSURE TO INVADE THE CONTINENT FROM THE SOVIET UNION, WHICH HAD BEEN TAKING ON THE BULK OF THE GERMAN ARMY SINCE THEY HAD INVADED IN 1941. THIS "FIRST FRONT," AS BRITAIN'S PRIME MINISTER WINSTON CHURCHILL LIKED TO CALL IT, DESPERATELY NEEDED HELP FROM THE NATIONS IN THE WEST. IF NOT, THE RUSSIANS MIGHT BE DEFEATED, THEN THE ENTIRE STRENGTH OF NAZI GERMANY COULD BE RELEASED AGAINST ENGLAND AND AMERICA.

MILLIONS WERE FIGHTING AND DYING ON THE RUSSIAN FRONT. SOVIET PREMIER JOSEPH STALIN CONSTANTLY DEMANDED THAT THE WESTERN NATIONS MOUNT A "SECOND FRONT." HE WAS TOLD THAT THIS WAS IMPOSSIBLE IN 1942. STALIN WOULD NOT ACCEPT THIS.

EVEN ENGLISH WORKERS, WHO FELT SOLIDARITY WITH THEIR RUSSIAN COMRADES, BECAME IMPATIENT WITH THE EXCUSES OF THE POLITICIANS AND GENERALS. SIGNS WENT UP ON STREETS AND IN FACTORIES ALL OVER ENGLAND.

BUT THE GENERALS AND THE POLITICIANS WERE RIGHT! IN AUGUST, 1942, 6,000 BRITISH AND CANADIAN TROOPS (WITH A HANDFUL OF U.S. RANGERS) LANDED ON THE FRENCH COAST AT DIEPPE. NEARLY 1,000 OF THE INVADERS WERE KILLED AND 2,000 CAPTURED. THE DIEPPE RAID WAS A COMPLETE FAILURE AND SILENCED THOSE CALLING FOR A PREMATURE INVASION. HOWEVER, THIS TRAGEDY TAUGHT THE WESTERN LEADERS MANY USEFUL LESSONS.

FIRST OF ALL, THEY LEARNED THAT THEY MUST HAVE ENOUGH MEN AND WEAPONS TO OVERWHELM THE DEFENDERS NO MATTER WHAT THE SITUATION. IN 1942, THE UNITED STATES WAS STILL IN THE PROCESS OF MOBILIZING.

ALSO, IT WOULD BE NECESSARY TO BUILD ENOUGH SHIPS TO CARRY AN INVASION FORCE. SPECIALLY DESIGNED LANDING CRAFT WERE STILL IN THE TESTING STAGES. IT WOULD BE A LONG TIME BEFORE THEY WOULD BE AVAILABLE IN THE NUMBERS REQUIRED.

ALTHOUGH THE MANPOWER AND MATERIALS WERE NOT YET AVAILABLE, THE ALLIES WENT RIGHT AHEAD WITH PLANNING. IN CHARGE WAS BRITISH GEN. SIR FREDERICK MORGAN.

WITH A HUGE, TALENTED STAFF BEHIND HIM, MORGAN CODE NAMED THE PLAN FOR THE INVASION OPERATION "OVERLORD."

HIS TEAM SPENT MANY GRUELING MONTHS GOING OVER EVERY ASPECT OF THE COMING INVASION. THEY HAD TO ANSWER THE KEY QUESTIONS: WHERE, WHEN, AND HOW.

THE *WHERE* FOR THE AMPHIBIOUS PART OF THE PLAN (CODE NAMED "NEPTUNE") WAS ONE OF THE MOST DIFFICULT PARTS OF THE PLAN. THE FINAL DECISION WOULD BE ONE OF THE MOST GUARDED SECRETS OF THE WAR.

ONLY 2 PLACES ON THE FRENCH COAST WERE SUITABLE FOR THE INVASION. THE PAS-DE-CALAIS SEEMED THE OBVIOUS CHOICE. HERE THE ENGLISH CHANNEL WAS AT ITS NARROWEST POINT. THIS WOULD MAKE THE SEA VOYAGE SHORT AND AIR COVER SIMPLER. ONCE LANDED THERE, THE ALLIED ARMIES WOULD HAVE THE SHORTEST AND MOST DIRECT ROUTE INTO GERMANY. HOWEVER, BECAUSE IT WAS THE MOST OBVIOUS, IT WAS ALSO THE MOST HEAVILY DEFENDED. THERE WERE ALSO HIGH CLIFFS OVERLOOKING NARROW BEACHES. THE NORMANDY COAST HAD NONE OF THESE DRAWBACKS. IT WAS LESS STRONGLY HELD, AND THE BEACHES WERE WIDE AND FIRM. ALSO, THE PORT OF CHERBOURG WAS NEARBY. A MAJOR PORT FOR THE MAMMOTH AMOUNT OF SUPPLIES NEEDED WAS CONSIDERED NECESSARY FOR SUCCESS.

IN DECEMBER, 1943, GEN. DWIGHT D. EISENHOWER WAS NAMED SUPREME COMMANDER OF THE INVASION FORCE. IKE, AS HE WAS CALLED BY HIS FRIENDS, WAS A TALENTED ADMINISTRATOR AND AN ABLE DIPLOMAT. THIS, AS AN AMERICAN, WAS NECESSARY TO HOLD THE DELICATE COALITION OF NATIONS TOGETHER. AROUND HIM, IKE GATHERED THE TOP MEN IN THEIR PROFESSIONS.

TO COMMAND OF THE SEA AND AIR ASPECTS OF THE INVASION, HE ASSIGNED 2 BRITS: ADM. SIR BERTRAM RAMSAY AND AIR CHIEF MARSHAL SIR ARTHUR TEDDER.

FOR THE OVERALL GROUND COMMANDER AND LEADER OF THE BRITISH FORCES, IKE PICKED GEN. SIR BERNARD L. MONTGOMERY, THE MAN WHO HAD DEFEATED GERMAN GEN. ERWIN ROMMEL AT EL ALAMEIN.

THIS WAS A DIFFICULT CHOICE. MONTGOMERY WAS VERY CRITICAL OF EISENHOWER'S DECISIONS AND THE AMERICANS IN GENERAL. IN FACT, HE WANTED IKE'S JOB FOR HIMSELF. THERE WAS A BIT OF IRONY IN HIS APPOINTMENT. THE GERMAN GENERAL FACING THEM ACROSS THE CHANNEL WAS NONE OTHER THAN ROMMEL HIMSELF, MONTGOMERY'S OLD NEMESIS. THE "DESERT FOX," AS ROMMEL WAS KNOWN, WOULD HAVE LIKED NOTHING BETTER THAN TO THROW HIS OLD FOE INTO THE ENGLISH CHANNEL AND HIS ARMY WITH HIM.

WHILE THE AMERICANS AND BRITISH WERE PLANNING THE INVASION, ROMMEL WAS DRIVING HIS TROOPS, ALONG WITH THOUSANDS OF SLAVE LABORERS, TO BUILD STRONGER AND STRONGER DEFENSES AND PLANT THOUSANDS AND THOUSANDS OF LAND MINES. BEHIND THE BEACHES, HE HAD LARGE AREAS FLOODED TO DROWN PARATROOPERS. HE DROVE LONG POLES INTO OPEN FIELDS TO THWART THE SAFE LANDING OF TROOP GLIDERS. HE ALSO PETITIONED HITLER TO BRING THE PANZER DIVISIONS AWAITING THE INVASION CLOSER TO THE COAST SO AN IMMEDIATE COUNTERATTACK COULD BE LAUNCHED AGAINST THE LANDING FORCE. HE FELT THAT FOR THE INVASION TO BE STOPPED, IT MUST BE DEFEATED ON THE BEACHES, WITHOUT GIVING THE ENEMY A CHANCE TO GET A TOEHOLD.

2 TOP AMERICAN GENERALS WERE IN ENGLAND FOR IMPORTANT JOBS IN THE INVASION. ONE WAS OMAR BRADLEY, WHO HAD FOUGHT SUCCESSFUL ACTIONS IN NORTH AFRICA AND SICILY. BRADLEY WAS TO COMMAND ALL AMERICAN FORCES IN THE INVASION AND THEN TAKE OVER COMMAND OF THE U.S. 1ST ARMY.

GENERAL GEORGE PATTON ALSO HAD AN IMPORTANT ROLE IN THE INVASION, BUT IT DIDN'T INVOLVE COMMANDING TROOPS. IN FACT, IT WAS QUESTIONABLE IF HE WOULD EVER COMMAND TROOPS AGAIN. HE HAD GOTTEN INTO TROUBLE IN SICILY FOR SLAPPING 2 G.I.S WHO WERE SUFFERING FROM BATTLE FATIGUE.

PATTON WAS IN ENGLAND TO COMMAND A "FALSE ARMY" OF EMPTY TENTS, RUBBER TANKS AND TRUCKS, AND FAKE RADIO TRAFFIC. THIS "PHANTOM ARMY" WAS LOCATED IN HIGHLY SECURED AREAS IN SOUTHEASTERN ENGLAND. ENOUGH INFORMATION ABOUT THIS FORCE WAS ALLOWED TO LEAK OUT SO THE GERMANS WOULD BELIEVE THAT PATTON WAS TO INVADE AT THE PAS-DE-CALAIS. HOPEFULLY, THIS RUSE WOULD KEEP MANY GERMAN DIVISIONS TIED UP WAITING FOR A LANDING THAT WOULD NEVER TAKE PLACE, FAR AWAY FROM NORMANDY.

THIS ASSIGNMENT WAS A DISAPPOINTMENT FOR PATTON. BUT HIS REAL ROLE IN THE INVASION WAS YET TO BE REVEALED.

THE *WHERE* OF THE INVASION HAD BEEN DECIDED, BUT WHAT ABOUT THE *WHEN?* ALL MATERIAL CONCERNS WOULD BE MET BY MAY 1, 1944. AFTER THAT, THE RIGHT WEATHER CONDITIONS WOULD BE NECESSARY. A LATE RISING MOON FOR THE AIRBORN ASSAULT. A LOW TIDE AT DAWN FOR THE AMPHIBIOUS ASSAULT. A FAIRLY CALM SEA FOR THE LANDING CRAFT. THIS WAS HARD TO PREDICT IN THE EVER-CHANGING ENGLISH CHANNEL.

OVERLORD'S METEOROLOGICAL BRAIN, CAPT. J. M. STAGG, CAUTIOUSLY PREDICTED EARLY JUNE, 1944.

ALL THROUGH THE MONTH OF MAY, MEN AND SUPPLIES MOVED SOUTH TO THE PORTS AND LOADING AREAS. MORE THAN 200,000 MEN WOULD BE INVADING THE CONTINENT ON THE FIRST DAY. IN THE DAYS AND WEEKS FOLLOWING THE INVASION, THOUSANDS AND THOUSANDS MORE WOULD BE FOLLOWING, ALONG WITH ALL THE AMMUNITION AND SUPPLIES THEY WOULD REQUIRE. OVER 6,000 SHIPS WOULD BE INVOLVED IN THIS ENORMOUS EFFORT.

FOR THE GREAT AIR OFFENSIVE, 163 BASES WERE BEING BUILT IN ADDITION TO THE SCORES OF U.S. AND ROYAL AIR FORCE FIELDS ALREADY IN EXISTENCE. SOME 11,000 COMBAT AIRCRAFT, 2,300 TRANSPORT AIRCRAFT, AND 2,600 GLIDERS WOULD BE AVAILABLE FOR THE INVASION FORCE. THE GERMANS IN FRANCE HAD LESS THAN 160 SERVICEABLE AIRCRAFT.

BEFORE THE INVASION, MOST OF THE FRENCH RAILROAD SYSTEM WOULD BE DESTROYED BY ALLIED AIRCRAFT OR BY SABOTAGE. THIS WOULD BE DONE TO KEEP GERMAN TROOPS FROM REINFORCING THE BEACHHEAD DEFENDERS. ALREADY IN ENGLAND WERE ALMOST 1,000 BRAND-NEW LOCOMOTIVES AND NEARLY 20,000 TANK CARS AND FREIGHT CARS TO REPLACE THEM. THESE WOULD BE USED TO MOVE SUPPLIES TO THE ADVANCING INVADERS.

EISENHOWER PUSHED BACK THE INVASION DATE FROM MAY (WHEN THE WEATHER HAD BEEN PERFECT) TO JUNE FOR ANOTHER MONTH'S PRODUCTION OF LANDING CRAFT. THE FIRST PERIOD OFFERING THE CORRECT COMBINATION OF MOON AND TIDE WAS JUNE 5, 6, AND 7, BUT THE WEATHER DETERIORATED TO SUCH A DEGREE THAT THE SCHEDULED DATE OF JUNE 5 HAD TO BE POSTPONED. IT LOOKED LIKE THE INVASION MIGHT HAVE TO BE DELAYED FOR ANOTHER MONTH. THAT COULD HAVE PUT THE SECURITY OF THE INVASION IN EXTREME JEOPARDY.

EISENHOWER AND HIS STAFF MET ON THE AFTERNOON OF MONDAY, JUNE 5. THE REPORT OF THE METEOROLOGIST STAGG WAS GLOOMY. HE STATED THAT IT WAS THE WORST WEATHER FOR THAT TIME OF YEAR IN 40 OR 50 YEARS. HOWEVER, HE PREDICTED AN IMPROVEMENT STARTING THAT AFTERNOON AND LASTING UNTIL LATE IN THE AFTERNOON OF THE NEXT DAY.

THAT EVENING, EISENHOWER WENT OUT TO THE HEADQUARTERS OF THE U.S. 101ST AIRBORNE DIVISION AT NEWBURY. HE SPENT AN HOUR TALKING TO THE MEN WHO WOULD BE DROPPING INTO FRANCE WITH THE U.S. 82ND AND BRITISH 6TH AIRBORNE DIVISIONS.

THAT WAS IT! ALL AT THE MEETING AGREED TO GO! EISENHOWER GAVE THE ORDER. TUESDAY, JUNE 6, 1944, WOULD BE D-DAY FOR THE INVASION.

AS THE HUGE FORMATIONS OF PLANES TOOK OFF FOR FRANCE, NBC CORRESPONDENT RED MUELLER LOOKED AT THE SUPREME COMMANDER. HE COULD SEE THERE WERE TEARS IN HIS EYES.

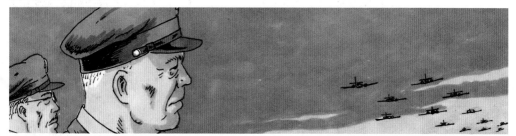

NORMANDY CHAPTER TWO HOW PEACEFUL THE LAND LOOKED

THE REASON FOR THE ALLIED AIRBORNE OPERATIONS WAS TO SECURE ROADS FOR EXITS OFF THE 5 LANDING BEACHES: UTAH, OMAHA, GOLD, JUNO, AND SWORD. IT WAS ALSO THE JOB OF THE PARATROOPERS TO SECURE CERTAIN ROADS TO KEEP GERMAN REINFORCEMENTS FROM COUNTERATTACKING THE BEACHES. THE AIRBORNE TROOPS EXPECTED HEAVY LOSES.

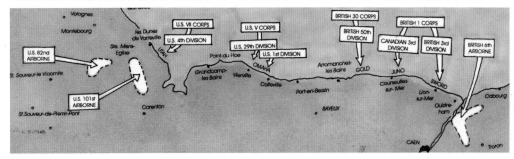

AT 0016, JUNE 6, THE BRITISH HORSA GLIDERS SILENTLY DESCENDED ON BÉNOUVILLE. THE 181 MEN ON BOARD WERE TO CAPTURE AND HOLD THE BRIDGE OVER THE CAEN CANAL.

THE MEN WERE MEMBERS OF THE OXFORDSHIRE AND BUCKINGHAMSHIRE LIGHT INFANTRY, AND THEIR COMMANDER WAS 31-YEAR-OLD MAJ. JOHN HOWARD. THESE MEN HAD BEEN TRAINING FOR SUCH A MISSION FOR MORE THAN 1 YEAR.

THE FIRST GLIDER TOUCHED DOWN AND SKIDDED INTO A BARBED WIRE FENCE. THIS SMASHED THE NOSE AND THREW THE PILOT AND CO-PILOT THROUGH THE COCKPIT, MAKING THEM THE FIRST ALLIED SOLDIERS ON FRENCH SOIL. NEVERTHELESS, THEY HAD BROUGHT THE GLIDER DOWN WITHIN A FEW YARDS OF THEIR OBJECTIVE, THE CANAL BRIDGE.

THE SECOND AND THIRD GLIDERS CAME RIGHT IN BEHIND THEM. WITHIN SECONDS, THEY DISGORGED THEIR OCCUPANTS, WHO POURED OUT OVER THE AREA. WITHIN 10 MINUTES, THESE MEN CAPTURED THE BRIDGE, KILLED THE GUARDS, AND DISARMED ANY DEMOLITIONS THAT THE GERMANS HAD PLACED. THEY THEN SETTLED IN TO HOLD THE BRIDGE FOR 2 HOURS UNTIL THE MAIN FORCE OF BRITISH PARATROOPERS COULD ARRIVE.

ALL OVER NORMANDY, PARATROOPERS OF THE U.S. 82ND AND 101ST AIRBORNE AND BRITISH 6TH AIRBORNE DIVISIONS WERE GETTING READY TO JUMP OUT OF C-47S. GEN. MATTHEW RIDGWAY, COMMANDING THE 82ND, LOOKED DOWN ON THE COUNTRYSIDE: "NO LIGHTS SHOWED... BUT IN THE PALE GLOW OF THE RISING MOON, I COULD CLEARLY SEE EACH FARM AND FIELD BELOW. HOW PEACEFUL THE LAND LOOKED, EACH HOUSE AND HEDGEROW, PATH AND LITTLE STREAM BATHED IN THE SILVER OF THE MOONLIGHT."

BUT IT WASN'T PEACEFUL. LOW CLOUDS AND FIRE FROM GERMAN GUNS CAUSED THE PLANES TO STRAY OFF THEIR COURSE.

BECAUSE OF THIS, MANY MEN CAME DOWN MILES FROM THEIR ASSIGNED DROP ZONES. SOME CAME DOWN ALONE IN THE DARK, LONELY FIELDS. STILL OTHERS LANDED IN THE AREAS FLOODED BY THE GERMANS AND QUICKLY DROWNED.

AT ABOUT 0130, IN THE TOWN OF STE.-MÈRE-ÉGLISE, THE TOWNSPEOPLE WERE OUT FIGHTING A FIRE STARTED BY ALLIED BOMBING. SUDDENLY, ALL FACES TURNED UPWARD AT THE SOUND OF LOW-FLYING PLANES.

A BATTALION OF THE 82ND AIRBORNE HAD MISSED ITS DROP ZONE AND WAS COMING DOWN IN THE MIDDLE OF THE TOWN SQUARE.

ILLUMINATED BY THE BURNING BUILDINGS, THE PARATROOPERS WERE PERFECT TARGETS FOR THE GERMANS IN THE SQUARE. THEY CAME DOWN AND GOT CAUGHT IN TREES AND ON THE ROOFS OF BUILDINGS. MANY HAD THEIR WEAPONS SECURED IN SPECIAL "LEG BAGS" AND WERE UNABLE TO REACH THEM. IT WAS A SLAUGHTER!

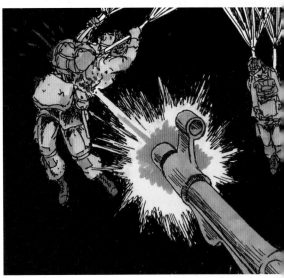

OTHER UNITS OF THE 82ND HAD MUCH BETTER LUCK. NOT FAR AWAY, BATTALION COMMANDER COL. BEN VANDERVOORT WAS OVERCOMING THE TROUBLES SUFFERED BY HIS OWN UNIT. HE HAD BROKEN HIS ANKLE IN THE DROP. DESPITE THIS, HE MANAGED TO GATHER 575 OF HIS ORIGINAL 630 MEN. BY DAWN, THEY HAD SECURED STE.-MÈRE-ÉGLISE, THE FIRST TOWN IN FRANCE TO BE LIBERATED BY THE AMERICANS.

BEHIND THE PARATROOPERS CAME REINFORCEMENTS AND HEAVY EQUIPMENT IN THE GLIDER TRAINS. TOWED BY C-47 DAKOTAS, EACH GLIDER COULD CARRY 34 FULLY EQUIPPED MEN UNLESS IT CARRIED VEHICLES OR LIGHT ARTILLERY. IT WAS A DANGEROUS WAY TO TRAVEL.

FIELD MARSHAL ROMMEL HAD EXPECTED GLIDER ATTACKS, SO HE HAD LONG POLES DRIVEN INTO THE GROUND IN OBVIOUSLY OPEN AREAS THAT WOULD MAKE GOOD LANDING FIELDS. THESE "ROMMEL'S ASPARAGUS" DID GREAT DAMAGE TO MANY GLIDERS. THE AMERICAN 101ST LOST 30 MEN IN GLIDER CRASHES. THE 82ND LOST NEARLY 300 IN THIS MANNER.

THE BRITISH 6TH AIRBORNE DIVISION HAD BETTER LUCK WITH BOTH THEIR PARATROOPERS AND THEIR GLIDERS. HOWEVER, THEY DID SUFFER THE LOSS OF IMPORTANT EQUIPMENT AND ARMS. A CASE IN POINT WAS THE VERY IMPORTANT ATTACK ON THE GERMAN GUN BATTERY AT MERVILLE. THE BATTERY WAS IN EASY RANGE OF BOTH JUNO AND SWORD BEACHES.

THE COMMANDER AND PLANNER OF THE RAID WAS LT. COL. TERENCE OTWAY. HE HAD DEVELOPED AN ELABORATE PLAN FOR TAKING THE BATTERY, BUT MOST OF THE EQUIPMENT WAS LOST IN THE DROP AND HE WAS ONLY ABLE TO GATHER 150 MEN OF HIS BATTALION OF 700!

OTWAY KNEW THE BATTERY HAD TO BE TAKEN NO MATTER WHAT. SO, WITH THE BLAST OF A BANGALORE TORPEDO RIPPING THROUGH THE GERMAN BARBED WIRE, THE BATTLE FOR THE MERVILLE BATTERY BEGAN.

THE PARATROOPERS CHARGED INTO THE SMOKE. THERE WERE SEVERAL EXPLOSIONS AND A SHARP CRY, "STOP! STOP! THERE ARE MINES EVERYWHERE!" BUT STILL THEY CHARGED ONWARD.

THE BATTLE WAS SHORT AND VIOLENT. 176 OF THE 200 GERMAN DEFENDERS WERE DEAD OR DYING. OTWAY LOST HALF OF HIS MEN. LIEUTENANT MIKE DOWLING, COVERED WITH BLOOD FROM A CHEST WOUND, REPORTED TO OTWAY, "BATTERY TAKEN, GUNS DESTROYED."

ALL OVER THE DARKENED COUNTRYSIDE, SMALL GROUPS OF MEN BANDED TOGETHER TO CARRY OUT MISSIONS THAT WERE INTENDED FOR MUCH LARGER, STRONGER FORCES. ONE OF THE MOST INCREDIBLE WAS THAT OF STAFF SGT. HARRISON SUMMERS OF THE 101ST AIRBORNE.

SUMMERS HAD BEEN GIVEN THE JOB OF CAPTURING A GERMAN COASTAL ARTILLERY BARRACKS DESIGNATED AS POINT WXYZ.

ACCOMPANIED BY PVT. JOHN CAMIEN AND AN UNKNOWN CAPTAIN FROM THE 82ND, SUMMERS CHARGED INTO THE STRONG POINT.

THE CAPTAIN WAS SOON KILLED, BUT MACHINE-GUNNER PVT. WILLIAM BURT JOINED IN THE FRAY BY GIVING COVERING FIRE. THE STUNNED GERMANS, ALTHOUGH CAUGHT BY SURPRISE, PUT UP A DEADLY SHIELD OF DEFENSIVE FIRE. IT DIDN'T SLOW SUMMERS DOWN.

SUMMERS BURST INTO ONE ROOM AND DISCOVERED 15 GERMANS SEATED AT A MESS TABLE EATING BREAKFAST. WITH HIS TOMMY GUN, SUMMERS CUT THEM DOWN. IN THE FIERY FIGHT, WHICH LASTED ALMOST 5 HOURS, SUMMERS AND HIS FRIENDS KILLED MORE THAN 100 GERMANS AND CAPTURED 31.

WHEN IT WAS ALL OVER, SUMMERS COLLAPSED FROM EXHAUSTION, HIS BODY BRUISED AND BLEEDING. A WITNESS OF HIS EXTRAORDINARY EXPLOITS ASKED HIM HOW HE FELT. "NOT VERY GOOD," HE ANSWERED. "IT WAS KIND OF CRAZY."

NORMANDY
CHAPTER THREE
HITTING THE BEACHES

JUNE 6, 1944, WAS A DAWN LIKE NO OTHER. IT WAS MURKY AND GRAY, BUT THE HUGE INVASION FLEET GAVE IT A MAJESTIC, FEARFUL GRANDEUR. AT 0550, JUST 10 MINUTES BEFORE SUNRISE, THE BIG WARSHIPS BEGAN THEIR PREPARATION BOMBARDMENT.

A FEW MINUTES LATER, A WAVE OF 276 B-26 MARTIN MARAUDERS SWEPT DOWN TO BOMB 7 DESIGNATED TARGETS. MOST OF THE BOMBS MISSED, FALLING SHORT INTO THE CHANNEL. IN FACT, MOST OF THE AIR BOMBARDMENT HAD BEEN A FAILURE. THE DEFENSES OF OMAHA BEACH HAD NOT BEEN SCRATCHED.

THE FIRST WAVE OF THE U.S. 4TH INFANTRY DIVISION TOUCHED DOWN ON UTAH BEACH AT 0630. WITH THEM WAS ONE OF THE MIRACLES OF THE INVASION, THE DD TANKS (DUPLEX DRIVE TANKS FITTED WITH A WORKING PROPELLER AND CONVERTIBLE SKIRTS THAT HELPED THEM KEEP AFLOAT).

WITH THE FIRST WAVE WAS THE 4TH'S ASSISTANT DIVISION COMMANDER, BRIG. GEN. THEODORE ROOSEVELT, JR. IT WAS HE WHO REALIZED THAT THEY HAD BEEN LANDED ON THE WRONG PART OF THE BEACH.

ROOSEVELT, JR., INSTRUCTED THE NAVY TO LAND THE SECOND AND THIRD WAVES RIGHT BEHIND THEM EVEN IF THEY WERE ON THE WRONG BEACH. THEN, HE DIRECTED THE 4TH TO MOVE INLAND. BY NOON, THEY HAD LINKED UP WITH THE 101ST AIRBORNE. BY NIGHTFALL, THEY HAD REACHED ALL THEIR D-DAY OBJECTIVES AT THE COST OF LESS THAN 20 DEAD AND 200 WOUNDED.

THINGS WERE NOT GOING WELL ON OMAHA BEACH. HIGH SEAS HAD SUNK MOST OF THE DD TANKS. WAVES WERE WASHING OVER INTO THE LANDING CRAFT, SINKING 32 AND CAUSING THE MEN IN THE OTHER BOATS TO BAIL. THE CURRENT WAS CARRYING THE BOATS OFF COURSE. SOME CRAFT STRUCK MINES.

OTHER BOATS, THEIR COXSWAINS TERRIFIED OF THE FIRE FROM THE BEACH, LET OUT THEIR HUMAN CARGO IN DEEP WATER. MANY OF THESE SOLDIERS, CARRYING AROUND 80 POUNDS OF EQUIPMENT, DROWNED WITHOUT FIRING A SHOT.

BUT THE WORST WAS YET TO COME. THE 13,000 BOMBS DROPPED ON OMAHA HAD MISSED THEIR TARGET BY 3 MILES! THE GERMAN 352ND DIVISION WAS WAITING AND READY FOR THE INVADERS TO COME IN WITH 4 BATTERIES OF ARTILLERY, 18 ANTI-TANK GUNS, 6 MORTAR PITS, 35 ROCKET LAUNCHER SITES, 8 CONCRETE BUNKERS, 35 PILLBOXES, AND 85 MACHINE-GUN NESTS. IT WAS GOING TO BE A LONG DAY ON OMAHA BEACH.

THE WEATHER WAS HAVING AN EFFECT ON GOLD BEACH TOO. THE SEA WAS TOO ROUGH TO RELEASE THE DD TANKS OUT AT SEA, SO THE LANDING CRAFT TANKS BRAVED THE GERMAN FIRE AND BROUGHT THEM RIGHT TO THE BEACH.

IN THE CENTER OF THE BRITISH 50TH INFANTRY DIVISION LANDING AREA WAS THE TOWN OF LE HAMEL. THERE THE GERMANS WERE PUTTING UP THEIR STRONGEST RESISTANCE. MANY OF THE BRITISH TANKS HAD BEEN KNOCKED OUT, AND A LARGE BARBED WIRE ENTANGLEMENT HAD NOT BEEN CLEARED BY THE ENGINEERS.

FORTUNATELY, A SINGLE FLAIL TANK (MOUNTED WITH A CHAIN SLINGING DEVICE TO CLEAR MINE FIELDS) HAD MADE IT ASHORE. IT MADE QUICK WORK OF THE BARBED WIRE AND OPENED THE WAY.

EAST OF LE HAMEL, THE 6TH GREEN HOWARDS LANDED. IN THE FRONT OF THEIR ADVANCE WAS COMMAND SGT. MAJ. STANLEY HOLLIS. A VETERAN OF DUNKIRK, NORTH AFRICA, AND SICILY, HOLLIS HAD KILLED 90 GERMANS SO FAR; HE INTENDED TO KILL MORE.

WITH A STEN GUN AND GRENADES, HOLLIS RUSHED A GERMAN PILLBOX. HE KILLED 2 OF ITS OCCUPANTS AND CAPTURED 20.

HOLLIS WOULD GO ON TO KILL MORE BEFORE THE DAY WAS OVER.

ON JUNO BEACH, THE LANDING OF THE CANADIAN 3RD INFANTRY DIVISION WAS DELAYED BECAUSE OF ROUGH WEATHER. SEVERAL OF THE DD TANKS DID MANAGE TO GET ASHORE ON THEIR OWN. LANDING CRAFT CARRYING TROOPS WERE BLOWN OFF COURSE AND CAME IN WITH MIXED UNITS. SEVERAL OF THE BOATS HAD THEIR BOTTOMS DAMAGED BY MINES, BUT ALL TROOPS GOT ASHORE SAFELY. JUST OFF THE BEACH WAS THE TOWN OF BERNIÈRES.

THE FIGHT FOR BERNIÈRES WAS BITTER, BUT BY MID-MORNING, IT WAS IN CANADIAN HANDS. IT WAS DISCOVERED THAT MANY OF THE "GERMAN" DEFENDERS WERE POLES OR RUSSIANS WHO HAD BEEN PRESSED INTO SERVICE. THEY USUALLY GAVE UP EASILY.

THE OBJECTIVE OF THE TROOPS COMING OFF JUNO BEACH WAS THE CITY OF CAEN, BUT GERMAN RESISTANCE STIFFENED AS THEY PUSHED INLAND, MAKING IT CLEAR THAT THEY WOULD NOT REACH THEIR OBJECTIVE.

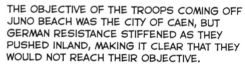

HOWEVER, THEY DID LINK UP WITH THE BRITISH 50TH COMING FROM GOLD BEACH.

SWORD BEACH WAS EXPECTED TO BE THE TOUGHEST OF THE 3 BRITISH BEACHES, AND TO THE MEN OF THE 2ND EAST YORK REGIMENT (PART OF THE BRITISH 3RD INFANTRY DIVISION), THIS PREDICTION SEEMED TO HOLD TRUE. THEY HIT THE BEACH IN THE FIRST WAVE.

ABOUT 150 OF THEIR BODIES LITTERED THE BEACH AND IT WAS A SHOCK TO THE MEN COMING IN AFTER THEM.

ONE OF THE UNITS IN THE FIRST WAVE WAS 176 MEN OF NUMBER 10 COMMANDO WHO WERE FREE FRENCH AND UNDER THE COMMAND OF COMMANDANT PHILIPPE VAISSEAU KIEFFER.

KIEFFER'S MEN ASSAULTED THE BEACH IN FRONT OF OUISTREHAM AND CAPTURED THE GERMAN STRONG POINT THERE. DE GAULLE'S FIGHTING FRENCH HAD ARRIVED.

ONE OF THE UNITS LANDING ON SWORD BEACH WAS LORD LOVAT'S 1ST BRIGADE, A 2,000-MAN COMMANDO UNIT WHOSE ASSIGNMENT WAS TO LINK UP WITH UNITS OF THE 6TH AIRBORNE.

SIMON CHRISTOPHER JOHN FRASER, THE 15TH LORD LOVAT OF SCOTLAND, HAD LED NO. 4 COMMANDO DURING THE DIEPPE RAID WITH SUCH DASH AND SKILL THAT HE LOST ONLY 12 OF HIS 252 MEN.

AT 1300, MAJOR HOWARD AND HIS MEN AT THE CAEN CANAL BRIDGE SUDDENLY HEARD BAGPIPES. IT WAS LORD LOVAT'S MEN THERE TO RELIEVE THEM. THE MEN THREW DOWN THEIR RIFLES, HUGGED EACH OTHER, AND THEN HUGGED LOVAT AND HIS MEN. MONSIEUR GEORGES GONDRÉE, THE OWNER OF A CAFÉ THAT HOWARD'S MEN WERE HOLDING, BROKE OUT A BOTTLE OF CHAMPAGNE. HIS WAS THE FIRST HOUSE LIBERATED ON D-DAY.

IN THE LAST HOURS OF D-DAY, 40 MARK IV TANKS OF THE 21ST PANZER DIVISION FOUGHT WITH SHERMAN TANKS OF THE STAFFORDSHIRE YEOMANRY. THE GERMANS LOST 8 TANKS AND WITHDREW. THE BRITISH WERE LESS THAN 3 MILES FROM CAEN, THEIR D-DAY OBJECTIVE. IT WOULD BE MANY WEEKS BEFORE THEY WOULD CROSS THOSE 3 MILES.

NORMANDY
CHAPTER FOUR
BLOODY OMAHA

SOMETIMES HISTORY CONFERS IMMORTALITY ON THE MOST ORDINARY OF PLACES. A HILL. A CHURCH. A CORN FIELD. ON D-DAY, IMMORTALITY WAS PLACED ON A 4-MILE STRETCH OF SAND CALLED OMAHA BEACH. IT WAS CHRISTENED IN BLOOD.

THE TROOPS WHO LANDED ON THE EASTERN HALF OF THE BEACH WERE OF THE 16TH REGIMENT OF THE 1ST INFANTRY DIVISION, A VETERAN OUTFIT THAT HAD FOUGHT HARD BATTLES IN NORTH AFRICA AND SICILY.

ON THE WESTERN HALF WAS THE 116TH REGIMENT OF THE 29TH INFANTRY DIVISION. THEY HAD BEEN SUPERBLY TRAINED, BUT THIS WAS THEIR FIRST FIGHT.

THE GERMAN FIRE ON THE BEACH WAS DEVASTATING. MEN WERE CUT DOWN WHILE STILL IN THEIR LANDING CRAFT. COMPANIES WERE LANDED FAR FROM THEIR ASSIGNED AREAS. CONFUSED AND LEADERLESS MEN HUDDLED BEHIND THE BEACH OBSTACLES, THEIR ONLY COVER. THEY SEEMED UNABLE OR UNWILLING TO ADVANCE FARTHER.

ESPECIALLY HARD HIT WERE THE 197 MEN OF A COMPANY OF THE 116TH. WITHIN THEIR FIRST 10 MINUTES ON OMAHA BEACH, 96 PERCENT OF THEM WERE KILLED OR WOUNDED. OF THE 35 MEN IN THE COMPANY FROM THE LITTLE TOWN OF BEDFORD, VIRGINIA, 20 WERE KILLED.

TO THE WEST OF OMAHA WERE THE CLIFFS OF POINTE DU HOC. THERE THE GERMANS HAD BUILT CASEMENTS FOR A BATTERY OF 6 155MM GUNS. THESE GUNS COULD HAVE SLAUGHTERED THE MEN ON OMAHA.

225 MEN OF THE 2ND RANGER BATTALION HAD BEEN GIVEN THE JOB OF TAKING THOSE GUNS OUT. THEY LANDED UNDER HEAVY FIRE ON THE NARROW BEACH JUST BELOW THE CLIFFS.

FROM THERE THEY FIRED ROCKET-PROPELLED GRAPPLING HOOKS WITH ATTACHED ROPES. THEN THEY BEGAN THE DANGEROUS CLIMB UP THE 9-STORY-HIGH CLIFF.

AS THEY CLIMBED THE CLIFF, THE DEFENDERS FIRED DOWN ON THEM AND THREW GRENADES. SOME OF THE GERMANS CUT THE ROPES FROM THE GRAPNELS, SENDING THE RANGERS TUMBLING BACK DOWN. BUT WITH HEAVY COVERING FIRE FROM THE DESTROYERS OFF SHORE, THE FIRST RANGERS MADE THE TOP WITHIN 5 MINUTES OF THE LANDING.

THE RANGERS FOUGHT ACROSS THE TOP OF THE CLIFF, TAKING ONE POSITION AFTER ANOTHER. THE FIGHT WAS COSTLY.

THE RANGERS FINALLY TOOK THE GUN CASEMENTS, ONLY TO DISCOVER THAT THE GUNS HAD NEVER BEEN INSTALLED. ONLY 90 OF THE ORIGINAL 225 RANGERS WERE STILL STANDING.

BACK ON OMAHA, SUCCESSIVE WAVES OF TROOPS HAD BEEN LANDED. FEW HAD GONE PAST THE BEACH OBSTACLES AND THE WATER'S EDGE WAS GETTING VERY CROWDED.

THE TIDE WAS NOW COMING IN 1 INCH EVERY MINUTE. BY 0800, THE TIDE HAD RISEN 8 FEET SINCE THE LANDING.

SOME MEN HAD ADVANCED AS FAR AS THE SHALE (THE FINE-GRAINED ROCK BAND BEYOND THE BEACH SAND), BUT THEY WERE BLOCKED BY A THICK BARBED WIRE.

THE FEW DD TANKS THAT DID MAKE IT ASHORE WERE QUICKLY KNOCKED OUT. THEIR PRESENCE COULD HAVE HELPED.

FOR THAT REASON, THE COMMANDERS OF THE LCTs DECIDED TO RUN THEIR CARGO OF TANKS RIGHT TO THE SAND DESPITE THE HEAVY GERMAN FIRE.

THE TANKS WERE LANDED, ADDING TO THE ALREADY HEAVY TRAFFIC PROBLEM. SOME WERE IMMEDIATELY KNOCKED OUT BY 88MM AND 75MM ANTI-TANK GUNS.

THE TANKS THAT MADE IT ASHORE BEGAN
TAKING ON THE JOB OF KNOCKING OUT GERMAN
GUN EMPLACEMENTS AND PILLBOXES.

GRADUALLY, THE MEN ON THE BEACH SHOOK
OFF THE SHOCK OF THEIR SURROUNDINGS,
GATHERED THEIR WITS AND THEIR WEAPONS,
AND BEGAN TO ADVANCE.

MEN TOOK ON THE MANTLE OF LEADERSHIP.
SOMETIMES THEY WERE OFFICERS. SOME OF
THEM WERE SERGEANTS OR EVEN PRIVATES.
THEY ENCOURAGED THE OTHERS TO FOLLOW.

BRIGADIER GENERAL NORMAN "DUTCH" COTA, 51-YEAR-OLD DEPUTY COMMANDER OF THE 29TH
DIVISION, WALKED UP AND DOWN THE BEACH, SOMETIMES EXPOSING HIMSELF TO ENEMY FIRE,
GIVING ORDERS AND ENCOURAGEMENT.

MEN LIKE COL. GEORGE A. TAYLOR, COMMANDER OF THE 1ST DIVISION'S 16TH REGIMENT, WERE THE ONES WHO MADE THE DIFFERENCE. THEY PUSHED, KICKED, PULLED, AND LED THEIR MEN OFF OMAHA BEACH. "2 KINDS OF PEOPLE ARE STAYING ON THIS BEACH," TAYLOR YELLED TO HIS MEN. "THE DEAD AND THOSE THAT ARE GOING TO DIE."

ONCE MOVING, THEY DIDN'T STOP. MEN STEPPED OVER THE BODIES OF THEIR FRIENDS AND FOUGHT THEIR WAY THROUGH THE DRAWS AND OVER THE RIDGES. IN SOME PLACES, IT TOOK 7 HOURS TO FIGHT THEIR WAY OFF THAT BEACH.

BY NIGHTFALL, THEY WERE 1 MILE INLAND, BUT THE COST HAD BEEN HIGH. OMAHA BEACH HAD COST 2,500 DEAD, WOUNDED, AND MISSING.

NORMANDY
CHAPTER FIVE
THE SKIN OF THEIR TEETH

ON THE SECOND DAY OF THE INVASION, JUNE 7, 1944, THE BRITISH AND AMERICAN FORCES BEGAN THE TREMEMDOUS TASK OF KEEPING THE TONS OF SUPPLIES FLOWING ASHORE. ON THAT DAY, THE U.S. 2ND INFANTRY DIVISION WAS LANDED. MANY, MANY MORE DIVISIONS WERE TO FOLLOW, BUT EVERONE KNEW THAT WITH EACH UNIT LANDED THE NEED FOR MORE AMMUNITION, FOOD, GASOLINE, AND OTHER ITEMS WOULD BE MULTIPLED.

THE USE OF PROPER PORT FACILITIES WAS PARAMOUNT, BUT IT WOULD BE WEEKS BEFORE CHERBOURG WOULD BE CAPTURED AND READY TO USE. SO THE ALLIES BROUGHT THEIR OWN PORT FACILITIES. IT WAS A REMARKABLE CONTRAPTION CALLED "MULBERRY." 2 OF THEM WERE BUILT IN ENGLAND, ONE FOR THE AMERICANS AND ONE FOR THE BRITISH. THEY WERE THEN FLOATED OVER AND ASSEMBLED JUST OFF THE INVASION BEACHES. A BREAKWATER WAS CREATED BY SINKING OLD SHIPS AND CONCRETE CAISSONS. EACH OF THESE ARTIFICIAL HARBORS WERE AS LARGE AS THE PORT OF DOVER!

ALSO, 3-INCH PIPE WAS LAID UNDER THE WATER FROM ENGLAND TO FRANCE TO PUMP FUEL FOR THE INVASION ARMY. OVER 1,000,000 GALLONS A DAY WERE PUSHED UNDER THE ENGLISH CHANNEL.

THE 2ND DIVISION WAS QUICKLY MOVED RIGHT INTO THE LINE BETWEEN THE 29TH AND THE 1ST DIVISIONS. EISENHOWER KNEW THAT THERE WAS NO TIME TO WASTE. THEY WERE IN A RACE WITH THE GERMANS TO SEE WHO COULD BRING UP THE MOST TROOPS THE QUICKEST. UNTIL THE BRITISH AND AMERICANS COULD BRING ENOUGH MEN AND EQUIPMENT TO OVERWHELM THE GERMANS, THEY WERE JUST HANGING ON BY THE SKIN OF THEIR TEETH.

THE MEN ALREADY THERE WERE CERTAINLY DOING THEIR PART. FOR EXAMPLE, GEN. "DUTCH" COTA SPENT JUNE 7 SHOWING A COMPANY OF THE 29TH HOW TO CAPTURE A GERMAN-OCCUPIED FARM HOUSE.

THE MEN OF THE 4TH/7TH ROYAL DRAGOON GUARDS SPENT THE DAY IN A BLOODY HOUSE-TO-HOUSE FIGHT FOR THE TOWN OF CREULLY.

HOWEVER, THE MEN OF THE INVASION ARMY WERE QUICKLY DISCOVERING ASPECTS OF THE NORMAN COUNTRYSIDE THAT WERE DEFINITELY IN THE FAVOR OF THE GERMANS. THE REGION WAS LOCALLY KNOWN AS THE *BOCAGE*. *BOCAGE* IS FRENCH FOR HEDGEROW. THE TROOPS WHO WERE TRAINED IN ENGLAND WERE USED TO THE LONG HEDGES THAT DIVIDED A FARMER'S FIELDS, BUT NOT HEDGES LIKE THESE. THE NORMAN HEDGES WERE ANCIENT ROWS OF EARTH 4 TO 6 FEET HIGH AND ABOUT 3 FEET THICK AT THE BASE. OUT FROM THESE ROWS OF EARTH GREW BUSHES AND TREES, THE ROOTS OF WHICH MADE IT ALMOST IMPOSSIBLE TO DIG INTO. THESE HEDGES PROTECTED THE FIELDS FROM THE HARSH ENGLISH CHANNEL WINDS.

EVERY SMALL FIELD AND PASTURE IN NORMANDY WAS DIVIDED THIS WAY AND USUALLY NOT IN JUST SQUARES BUT IN TRIANGLES AND RECTANGLES. THERE WERE FEW STRAIGHT LINES. THE ROADS AND HEDGES TWISTED AND TURNED.

THEY WERE SUNKEN BY EROSION AND WEAR. THE TREES GROWING OVER THEM, ENTANGLING WITH THOSE ON THE OTHER SIDE, FORMED LEAFY CAVES.

EACH SMALL FIELD WAS ACCESSIBLE BY A SINGLE WOODEN GATE, EASILY DEFENDED BY A FEW MEN.

THE NARROW ROADS WERE DEATH TRAPS FOR ALLIED TANKS. IF THEY TRIED TO CLIMB OVER THE HEDGEROW, EXPOSING THEIR THINLY ARMORED BELLIES TO GERMAN ANTI-TANK WEAPONS LIKE THE PANZERFAUST...

THIS SORT OF FIGHTING WAS TOTALLY ALIEN TO THE YOUNG AMERICAN G.I.S, AND LEARNING IT WAS VERY COSTLY.

ON THE NIGHT OF JUNE 9, A BATTALION FROM THE 29TH, EXHAUSTED FROM FIGHTING AND MARCHING, BIVOUACKED IN A HEDGED FIELD WITHOUT DIGGING FOXHOLES OR EVEN PUTTING OUT SENTRIES.

AT ABOUT 0200 THE NEXT MORNING, THE SLEEPING MEN WERE ATTACKED BY GERMANS SUPPORTED BY STURMGESCHÜTZE (ASSAULT GUNS, BASICALLY TANKS WITHOUT TURRETS). IT WAS A SLAUGHTER. ABOUT 50 MEN WERE KILLED AND 100 MORE WOUNDED AND CAPTURED. THE REST OF THE BATTALION WAS SCATTERED ALL OVER THE COUNTRYSIDE.

THE NATURE OF THE COUNTRYSIDE DICTATED TO THE GERMANS HOW THEY WOULD DEPLOY THEIR TROOPS. THE AMERICAN 1ST ARMY (UNDER GENERAL BRADLEY) ENCOUNTERED THE HEAVIEST CONCENTRATION OF *BOCAGE*. HERE ROMMEL WOULD HOLD THE LINE WITH REGULAR INFANTRY. HOWEVER, THE AREA IN FRONT OF MONTGOMERY'S BRITISH 2ND ARMY WAS ROLLING, OPEN FARMLAND, IDEAL FOR TANKS. IT WAS HERE THAT ROMMEL WOULD CONCENTRATE HIS PANZER DIVISIONS. BUT ROMMEL HAD 2 PROBLEMS KEEPING HIM FROM DOING THIS. 1 WAS ALLIED AIR POWER. THE OTHER WAS ADOLF HITLER.

HITLER'S PROBLEM WAS THAT HE BELIEVED THE LANDING IN NORMANDY (THE AREA DEFENDED BY THE GERMAN 7TH ARMY) WAS JUST A DECEPTION AND THAT THE REAL INVASION WOULD TAKE PLACE AT THE PAS-DE-CALAIS (WHERE THE GERMAN FIFTEENTH ARMY WAS LOCATED, WITH THE BULK OF THE PANZER DIVISIONS). HE WOULD NOT ALLOW ROMMEL TO TRANSFER THESE UNITS TO MEET THE THREAT IN NORMANDY. EVEN WITH THE INSISTENCE OF ROMMEL'S SUPERIOR, FIELD MARSHALL VON RUNDSTEDT, HITLER WOULD NOT RELEASE THESE UNITS.

3 STRONG PANZER DIVISIONS WERE ALREADY NEAR THE BEACHHEAD OR IN THE AREA: THE 21ST PANZER, PANZER LEHR, AND THE 12TH SS PANZER "HITLERJÜGEND." VON RUNDSTEDT MANAGED TO GET 3 OTHER PANZER DIVISIONS ASSIGNED TO NORMANDY: 2ND PANZER, 1ST SS PANZER "LAH," AND 2ND SS PANZER "DAS REICH," WHICH WERE MILES AWAY IN OTHER PARTS OF FRANCE. HE ALSO MANAGED TO GET THE 9TH AND 10TH SS TRANSFERRED FROM THE RUSSIAN FRONT. FOR ALL THESE UNITS, THE MOVEMENT TO NORMANDY WOULD TAKE DAYS, EVEN WEEKS, AND WOULD BE VERY HAZARDOUS.

THIS IS WHERE THE PROBLEM OF ALLIED AIR POWER CAME IN. BRITISH AND AMERICAN PLANES HAD SUCH COMPLETE CONTROL OF THE AIR THAT ALL MOVEMENT ON THE GROUND DURING DAYLIGHT HOURS BROUGHT FIGHTER BOMBERS SWARMING IN LIKE ANGRY HORNETS.

ANY MOVEMENT TO THE FRONT FOR THESE UNITS HAD TO BE AT NIGHT. OTHERWISE, THEY WOULD BE BOMBED AND STRAFED BY HAWKER TYPHOONS OR P-47 THUNDERBOLTS.

THE THREAT FROM THE AIR WAS SO BAD THAT GERMAN TANK CREWS BEGAN COMPLETELY COVERING THEIR VEHICLES WITH GREENERY FROM THE SURROUNDING LANDSCAPE. A PANTHER TANK THAT NORMALLY LOOKED LIKE THIS...

...LOOKED LIKE THIS!

THERE WAS ANOTHER ELEMENT THAT COULD DELAY THESE GERMAN UNITS IN THEIR MARCH TO THE BATTLEFIELD: THE FRENCH RESISTANCE. THEY SO HAMPERED THE 2ND SS IN THEIR JOURNEY FROM SOUTHERN FRANCE THAT A TRIP THAT WOULD NORMALLY TAKE SEVERAL DAYS TOOK 2 WEEKS.

THIS HARASSMENT WAS NOT WITHOUT COST TO THE RESISTANCE OR TO INNOCENT FRENCH CIVILIANS. THE 2ND SS PANZER DAS REICH, A HARDCORE NAZI OUTFIT, DECIDED TO TAKE OUT THEIR ANGER ON THE LITTLE TOWN OF ORADOUR-SUR-GLANE, POPULATION 642. THERE THEY MURDERED EVERY MAN, WOMAN, AND CHILD.

MORE AND MORE ALLIED UNITS WERE POURING ACROSS THE BEACHES AND INTO THE LINES. IN FACT, MONTGOMERY WAS ABOUT TO MAKE A MAJOR BID TO CAPTURE CAEN. TO DO IT, HE BROUGHT IN A LEGENDARY OUTFIT TO SMASH THROUGH THE GERMAN DEFENSE.

WHAT MONTGOMERY DIDN'T COUNT ON WAS THAT THE GERMANS HAD A LEGEND OF THEIR OWN TO STOP HIM.

NORMANDY
CHAPTER SIX
THE TIGERS OF VILLERS-BOCAGE

CAEN WAS A MAJOR OBJECTIVE OF MONTGOMERY'S BRITISH 2ND ARMY. THERE WAS AN
AIRFIELD WEST OF THE CITY AT CARPIQUET THAT WAS STRONGLY DEFENDED BY THE 12TH SS.
BUT THE REAL REASON FOR THE GERMANS HOLDING CAEN WAS TO KEEP THE ALLIES OUT OF
THE COUNTRY BEYOND IT. FOR ONCE ONE PASSED CAEN, THE COUNTRY WAS OPEN WITH GENTLY
ROLLING FARM LAND, IDEAL FOR TANKS, ALL THE WAY TO PARIS.

THE GERMAN DEFENSIVE LINE EXTENDED WEST FROM CAEN, BEYOND THE SECTOR OF
THE 12TH SS, THROUGH THE LINE HELD BY THE PANZER LEHR DIVISION. THERE THE LINE
EFFECTIVELY ENDED IN THE BEGINNING OF THE HEAVY HEDGEROW COUNTRY. THERE THE
MOVEMENT OF ARMORED FORCES WAS MORE RESTRICTED. OR SO THE GERMANS BELIEVED.

IT WAS AT THE END OF THIS LINE THAT MONGOMERY PLANNED TO LAUNCH AN ATTACK TO FLANK
THE GERMAN DEFENSES. FOR THIS HE WAS BRINGING IN A FRESH BUT HIGHLY EXPERIENCED
ARMORED DIVISION. THIS DIVISION HAD WON FAME IN THE NORTH AFRICAN DESERT AS "THE
DESERT RATS"—THE BRITISH 7TH ARMORED DIVISION. IT WAS A GOOD PLAN, BUT THERE WERE
THINGS THAT MONTGOMERY DID NOT KNOW.

THE BRITISH BEGAN THEIR ADVANCE ON TUESDAY, JUNE 12. UNKNOWN TO THEM, LEAD ELEMENTS OF THE GERMAN 101ST HEAVY TANK BATTALION BEGAN TO ARRIVE IN THE AREA. THIS UNIT HAD SEEN A LOT OF ACTION ON THE RUSSIAN FRONT.

THIS BATTALION'S 2ND COMPANY MOVED INTO A WOODED AREA JUST NORTHEAST OF THE VILLAGE OF VILLERS-BOCAGE. THEIR 37 TIGER TANKS WERE CAMOUFLAGED BY THEIR CREWS.

THE NEXT MORNING, JUNE 13, THE COMMANDER OF THE 2ND COMPANY MOVED HIS TIGER OUT TOWARD THE VILLAGE TO RECONNOITER. HE SPOTTED THE LEAD ELEMENTS OF THE BRITISH 7TH ARMORED DIVISION IN THE VILLAGE OUTSKIRTS.

THE COMMANDER OF THE 2ND COMPANY WAS NO ORDINARY TANKER. HE WAS MICHAEL WITTMANN, A LEGENDARY PANZER LEADER WHOSE CREW HAD DESTROYED 117 RUSSIAN TANKS.

WITTMANN'S TIGER CHARGED ONTO THE ROAD, TOOK A HARD LEFT, AND FACED 4 TANKS OF THE BRITISH 22ND ARMORED BRIGADE. THE BRITS WERE COMPLETELY SURPRISED.

IN QUICK SUCCESSION, WITTMANN'S TIGER BLASTED ALL 4 OF THE BRITISH TANKS.

HE THEN DIRECTED HIS DRIVER TO ADVANCE DOWN A HILL AND INTO THE TOWN.

IN DOING SO, HE PASSED THE CROMWELL TANK OF CAPT. PAT DYAS, WHICH HAD WISELY BACKED OFF THE ROAD INTO A LITTLE GARDEN. DYAS AND HIS CREW WATCHED HELPLESSLY AS WITTMANN'S TANK PASSED.

WITTMANN SPOTTED A COLUMN OF BRITISH TANKS COMING IN FROM THE OTHER SIDE OF TOWN. THEY WERE "FIREFLIES," AMERICAN SHERMAN TANKS ARMED WITH 17-POUNDER GUNS, CAPABLE OF DESTROYING A TIGER TANK. WITTMANN WISELY ORDERED HIS DRIVER TO TURN AROUND AND HEAD BACK THE WAY THEY CAME.

AS THEY RETRACED THEIR TRACKS, THEY CAME FACE-TO-FACE WITH DYAS'S CROMWELL, WHICH HAD COME OUT OF THE GARDEN TO STOP THEM.

THE TIGER MADE QUICK WORK OF THE CROMWELL. DYAS MANAGED TO ESCAPE ON FOOT, BUT HIS CREW WAS DONE FOR.

WITTMANN'S TIGER PASSED DYAS'S BURNING VEHICLE, TOOK A LEFT, AND CLIMBED A HILL OUTSIDE OF TOWN. FROM THERE, HE COULD SEE A LONG COLUMN OF TANKS, VEHICLES, AND A COMPANY OF THE 1ST REGIMENT, 7TH ARMORED. WITTMANN'S 88MM GUN WENT TO WORK ON THEM.

WITTMAN RIGHT AWAY BEGAN SHOOTING UP THE VEHICLES OF THE STAFF COMPANY.

HIS TIGER THEN ROLLED FORWARD AND, USING A HEDGE FOR COVER, KNOCKED OUT THE TANKS OF "A" COMPANY.

WITH FLAME AND DESTRUCTION BEHIND HIM, WITTMANN ROLLED BACK INTO VILLERS-BOCAGE. BY NOW, HE HAD BEEN CONTACTED BY A GROUP OF TANKS FROM HIS UNIT, WHICH WAS ON ITS WAY TO JOIN HIM IN THE FIGHT.

BUT THIS TIME WOULD BE DIFFERENT. BRITISH TANKS AND ANTI-TANK GUNS WERE IN THE TOWN. THEY KNEW THAT WITTMANN WOULD BE BACK, AND THEY SET UP AN AMBUSH.

WHEN WITTMANN'S TIGER ROLLED BACK DOWN THE STREET, 4 TANKS UNDER THE COMMAND OF LT. BILL COTTON OPENED FIRE. A FATAL SHOT WENT INTO THE HEAVY TANK'S SIDE, AND WITTMANN AND HIS CREW BEGAN TO BAIL OUT.

AS WITTMANN AND HIS
CREW RAN FOR COVER,
THE OTHER TIGER TANKS
CHARGED ON DOWN THE
STREET, FIRING AT THE
BRITISH TANKS AND
GUN POSITIONS.

THEY, TOO, WERE FINALLY
DESTROYED, BUT NOT
AFTER INFLICTING
MAXIMUM DAMAGE.

FIGHTING CONTINUED IN VILLERS-BOCAGE UNTIL DARK. THE BRITISH 7TH ARMORED DIVISION
HAD TO CALL OFF THEIR ATTACK ON CAEN. MICHAEL WITTMANN AND THE OTHER MEN OF THE
101ST HEAVY TANK BATTALION HAD DESTROYED 27 TANKS AND JUST AS MANY HALF-TRACKS AND
TRUCKS. THE TIP OF THE BRITISH ATTACK HAD BEEN BROKEN.

NORMANDY

CHAPTER SEVEN

DEATH IN THE HEDGEROWS

SATURDAY, JUNE 17. FIELD MARSHAL ROMMEL AND VON RUNDSTEDT MET WITH HITLER AT SOISSONS. BOTH MILITARY LEADERS WANTED TO WITHDRAW BEHIND A BETTER POSITION. HITLER, AS HE HAD DONE SO MANY TIMES IN RUSSIA, DEMANDED THAT "NOT A SINGLE INCH OF GROUND BE GIVEN UP." ROMMEL AND VON RUNDSTEDT ALSO REQUESTED THE MOVING OF THE PANZER DIVISIONS FROM THE 15TH ARMY TO THE NORMANDY AREA. HITLER ALSO REJECTED THIS. HE WAS STILL CERTAIN THAT THE NORMANDY LANDING WAS JUST AN ALLIED RUSE AND THAT THE REAL INVASION WOULD COME AT THE PAS-DE-CALAIS.

MORE AND MORE AMERICAN DIVISIONS WERE COMING IN TO FORM A NEW U.S. CORPS. THE XIX CORPS BECAME OPERATIONAL BETWEEN VII AND V CORPS. THE VII CORPS, UNDER GEN. LAWTON COLLINS, HAD THE JOB OF PUSHING NORTH TOWARD CHERBOURG.

ON THE SAME DAY THAT ROMMEL, VON RUNDSTEDT, AND HITLER WERE HAVING THEIR CONFERENCE, THE U.S. 9TH INFANTRY DIVISION REACHED THE WEST COAST OF THE COTENTIN PENINSULA, EFFECTIVELY CUTTING OFF ALL THE GERMANS IN CHERBOURG.

COLLINS HAD LED TROOPS IN THE PACIFIC AGAINST THE JAPANESE. HE WOULD GO ON TO BECOME THE ARMY'S CHIEF OF STAFF.

THE GERMAN COMMANDER OF CHERBOURG, GENERAL VON SCHLIEBEN, EXECUTED A FIGHTING WITHDRAWAL AS HE BACKED OFF INTO THE FORTIFIED BAND AROUND THE PORT.

HE HAD 25,000 TROOPS AT HIS DISPOSAL, BUT THEY WERE OF QUESTIONABLE QUALITY. INCLUDED WERE POLICEMEN, SAILORS, AND CLERKS. 20 PERCENT WERE POLES, RUSSIANS, AND ITALIANS, THE PRODUCT OF NAZI CONQUEST. HE WAS ALSO SHORT OF FOOD, SUPPLIES, AND AMMUNITION.

ON JUNE 20, THE U.S. 9TH, 79TH, AND 4TH INFANTRY DIVISIONS REACHED THE DEFENSIVE COMPLEX THAT SURROUNDED CHERBOURG. MASSIVE CONCRETE PILLBOXES, UNDERGROUND AMMUNITION STORAGE FACILITIES, CONNECTING TRENCHES, AND BARBED WIRE BARRIERS STOOD IN THE WAY. INITIAL ATTACKS RESULTED IN SHARP FIGHTS AND HEAVY CASUALTIES.

TRYING TO AVOID A BLOODY FRONTAL ASSAULT, COLLINS CALLED IN THE AIR FORCE. ON JUNE 22, HUNDREDS OF FIGHTER-BOMBERS ATTACKED THE STRONG POINTS. THESE ATTACKS DID NOT PULVERIZE THE FORTIFICATIONS, BUT THEY DID SHAKE THE MORALE OF THE MEN INSIDE THEM.

WHEN THE AMERICAN ATTACKS RESUMED ON JUNE 23, THEY BEGAN TO MAKE HEADWAY.

VON SCHLIEBEN INFORMED HITLER THAT THEY COULD NOT HOLD OUT MUCH LONGER. HITLER SAID, "IF WORSE COMES TO WORSE, IT IS YOUR DUTY TO DEFEND THE LAST BUNKER AND LEAVE THE ENEMY NOT A HARBOR, BUT A FIELD OF RUINS."

LIKE ALL WARS BEFORE AND SINCE, AIR POWER ITSELF COULD NOT DO THE JOB. WHEN THE SMOKE CLEARED, IT WAS TIME FOR THE FOOT SOLDIER TO MOVE UP AND DIG THE ENEMY OUT OF THEIR HOLES. THE 79TH DIVISION CAME UP AGAINST FORT DU ROULE ON JUNE 25.

IN THIS FIGHT, CPL. JOHN D. KELLY KNOCKED OUT A PILLBOX WITH POLE CHARGES AND GRENADES. KELLY DIED OF WOUNDS IN THE SUBSEQUENT ACTION.

FIRST LIEUTENANT CARLOS C. OGDEN, ALTHOUGH BADLY WOUNDED, CAPTURED AN 88MM GUN THAT WAS BLOCKING HIS COMPANY'S ADVANCE.

BOTH KELLY AND OGDEN WERE AWARDED THE MEDAL OF HONOR.

ON JUNE 26, THE GERMAN GARRISON IN CHERBOURG SURRENDERED, BUT THE PORT WAS IN A SHAMBLES. AS HITLER HAD ORDERED, VON SCHLIEBEN HAD DONE AS MUCH DAMAGE AS POSSIBLE. THE ARMY ENGINEERS AND NAVY SALVAGE TEAMS WENT TO WORK. ON JULY 16, JUST 3 WEEKS AFTER ITS CAPTURE, THE PORT BEGAN TO ACCEPT ALLIED SHIPS.

WHILE THE CAPTURE OF CHERBOURG WAS IN PROGRESS, THE SOUTHERN ADVANCE HAD STAGNATED IN THE HEAVY HEDGEROW COUNTRY. BUT EVEN THOUGH THERE HAD BEEN NO ADVANCE DIDN'T MEAN THERE WEREN'T ANY CASUALTIES. THERE WERE CONSTANT SKIRMISHES THAT WERE JUST AS DEADLY TO THE MEN ON THE FRONT AS ANY MAJOR OFFENSIVE. FOR EXAMPLE, IN THE 29TH DIVISION, CASUALTIES HAD BEEN SO HEAVY THAT MANY COMPANIES HAD ONLY A HANDFUL LEFT OF THOSE WHO HAD LANDED ON D-DAY. IT DIDN'T HELP THAT THE GERMAN 3RD FALLSCHIRMJÄGER (GERMAN PARATROOPERS) HELD PART OF THE LINE IN FRONT OF THEM. THEY WERE TOUGH OPPONENTS.

THE OBJECTIVE HAD ALWAYS BEEN ST.-LÔ, WHERE 8 MAJOR ROADS CAME TOGETHER AND THE BOCAGE COUNTRY BEGAN TO OPEN UP A LITTLE. ST.-LÔ WAS ONLY ABOUT 20 MILES FROM OMAHA BEACH AS THE CROW FLIES. BUT ALLIED SOLDIERS WERE NOT CROWS.

THE U.S. ARMY REPLACEMENT SYSTEM WAS FAR FROM PERFECT. GROUP OR EVEN SINGLE REPLACEMENTS WOULD COME THROUGH A REPLACEMENT DEPOT FREQUENTLY CALLED A "REPPLE DEPPLE."

THEY WOULD BE SENT TO A UNIT WHICH HAD SUFFERED CASUALTIES, NOT KNOWING ANYONE OR HAVING ANY FRIENDS THERE. IF THEY WERE LUCKY, THEY WOULD REACH THEIR NEW UNIT WHILE IT WAS IN A RESERVE OF REST AREA.

IF THEY WERE UNLUCKY, THEY WOULD REACH THEM WHILE THEY WERE IN COMBAT.

MANY REPLACEMENTS WERE TREATED IN A LESS-THAN-WELCOME MANNER. SOME VETERANS WERE RESENTFUL THAT THE NEW MAN MAY HAVE BEEN REPLACING A GOOD FRIEND. THE VETERAN DIDN'T WANT TO GET TO KNOW THE "NEW MAN." THEY DIDN'T REALLY BELIEVE HE WOULD BE AROUND LONG ENOUGH TO GET TO KNOW VERY WELL.

MANY A REPLACEMENT WOULD REACH A UNIT AND BE KILLED OR SERIOUSLY WOUNDED WITHIN HOURS OF GETTING THERE. FEW OF HIS VETERAN COMRADES WOULD EVEN GET TO KNOW HIS NAME. IT WAS A VERY LONELY WAY TO DIE.

STILL, IF A REPLACEMENT MANAGED TO SURVIVE HIS FIRST 24 HOURS ON THE LINE, HE WAS A REGULAR "DOG-FACE," A COMBAT SOLDIER. IN A FEW DAYS, HE WOULD BE ACCEPTED AS ONE OF THE REGULAR GROUP.

BY JULY 1, 11 AMERICAN INFANTRY DIVISIONS MANNED THE LINE BETWEEN THE BRITISH 2ND ARMY IN THE EAST AND THE WESTERN COAST OF THE COTENTIN PENINSULA. EACH DIVISION HAD ABOUT 15,500 MEN. ASIDE FROM MANY SUPPORT UNITS, EACH DIVISION HAD 3 INFANTRY REGIMENTS. EACH REGIMENT HAD 3 BATTALIONS. EACH BATTALION HAD 3 INFANTRY COMPANIES AND 1 HEAVY WEAPONS COMPANY.

EACH INFANTRY COMPANY HAD ABOUT 200 MEN AT FULL STRENGTH (WHICH THEY HARDLY EVER WERE). THEY WERE COMMANDED BY A CAPTAIN, WITH A 1ST LIEUTENANT AND A 1ST SERGEANT ("TOP KICK") TO ASSIST HIM.

EACH COMPANY HAD 3 RIFLE PLATOONS AND 1 WEAPONS PLATOON. THE RIFLE PLATOON HAD ABOUT 45 MEN, COMMANDED BY A 2ND LIEUTENANT AND A PLATOON SERGEANT.

EACH PLATOON HAD 3 SQUADS OF 12 MEN COMMANDED BY A BUCK SERGEANT WITH A CORPORAL TO ASSIST HIM.

EACH SQUAD ALSO HAD A BAR (BROWNING AUTOMATIC RIFLE) MAN AND AN ASSISTANT TO HELP HIM CARRY AMMO.

EACH SQUAD HAD 8 RIFLEMEN, EACH ARMED WITH THE M-1 GARAND. THIS SEMI-AUTOMATIC RIFLE WAS WITHOUT A DOUBT THE BEST PERSONAL WEAPON OF THE WAR. IT COULD FIRE 8 30.06 CALIBER ROUNDS AS FAST AS A MAN COULD PULL THE TRIGGER.

HOWEVER, THE GERMANS HAD THEM OUTGUNNED IN SOME AREAS. THE U.S. BROWNING 30-CALIBER MACHINE GUN WAS NO MATCH FOR THE MG 42. IT SEEMED LIKE THE GERMANS HAD MORE OF THEM TOO.

THE GERMAN PERSONAL ANTI-TANK WEAPONS WERE BETTER AS WELL. PANZERFAUST AND THE PANZERSCHRECK WERE BOTH BETTER THAN THE BAZOOKA. THE GERMANS ALSO HAD MAGNETIC ANTI-TANK GRENADES AND WERE WELL TRAINED IN THEIR USE.

THE GERMAN 88MM WAS ONE OF THE MOST-FEARED WEAPONS OF WORLD WAR II. BUT AS THE ALLIES LANDED MORE AND MORE ARTILLERY, THE BALANCE BEGAN TO SHIFT IN THEIR FAVOR. THE MAIN THING WAS THE EVER-PRESENT ALLIED AIR SUPERIORITY. THE GERMANS COULD NOT HOPE TO MATCH THAT AND, IN THE END, THIS WAS WHAT REALLY MATTERED.

NORMANDY
CHAPTER EIGHT
THE DEVIL'S CHILDREN

THE CENTER OF THE GERMAN LINE IN FRONT OF CAEN WAS HELD BY THE 12TH SS PANZER DIVISION, ALSO CALLED THE HITLERJÜGEND (HITLER YOUTH) DIVISION. IT WAS A MOST UNUSUAL UNIT. IN FACT, IT CAN BE SAFELY STATED THAT IT WAS ONE OF THE TOUGHEST AND MOST COURAGEOUS DIVISIONS OF WORLD WAR II...AND ONE OF THE MOST BRUTAL.

THE DIVISION WAS FORMED IN 1943 FROM 16- AND 17-YEAR-OLD RECRUITS FROM THE HITLER YOUTH. THIS WAS SORT OF THE NAZI VERSION OF BOY SCOUTS. INSTEAD OF LEARNING CAMPING CRAFT AND KNOT TYING, THEY LEARNED RACIAL STEREOTYPING AND MILITARY WEAPONS HANDLING.

MORE THAN 20,000 OF THESE YOUTH REPORTED TO LICHTERFELDE KASERNE IN BERLIN FOR THIS NEW DIVISION. THE MOTHERS OF GERMANY WERE SAYING A PROUD GOODBYE TO THEIR SONS...

...THEY WOULD NOT SEE THEM AGAIN.

THE OFFICER, NCO, AND TRAINING CADRE CAME FROM THE 1ST SS PANZER DIVISION, THE LEIBSTANDARTE (BODYGUARD). THIS UNIT TRACED ITS LINEAGE BACK TO A SMALL GROUP OF MEN WHO GUARDED ADOLF HITLER IN THE EARLY DAYS OF THE PARTY. IN 1943, THESE MEN HAD JUST COME BACK FROM 2 HARD YEARS OF FIGHTING ON THE RUSSIAN FRONT.

THE TRAINING OF THE HITLERJÜGEND (HJ) WAS DIFFERENT THAN ANY OTHER UNIT IN THE GERMAN ARMY. MARCHING AND DRILLING WERE DROPPED ALTOGETHER. EVERYTHING WAS FOCUSED ON PREPARING FOR BATTLE USING ALL THE DIRTY TRICKS THAT THE LEIBSTANDARTE HAD LEARNED IN RUSSIA. THEIR MOTTO WAS, "TRAINED NOT AS SOLDIERS, BUT AS FIGHTERS."

SMOKING AND DRINKING WERE FORBIDDEN. RELATIONSHIPS WITH GIRLS WERE PROHIBITED TO THOSE UNDER 18. HOWEVER, THE NCOS HAD PLENTY OF CANDY ON HAND TO PASS OUT. MILITARY RANK WAS LOOKED ON QUITE DIFFERENTLY. THE OFFICERS AND NCOS WERE MORE LIKE EXPERIENCED BIG BROTHERS AND CONSIDERED MORE LIKE CHAMPIONS AND CLOSE FRIENDS.

THE 22,000-MAN DIVISION THAT ARRIVED IN NORMANDY IN 1944 WAS SOMETHING TO SEE. THEIR HAIR WAS LONGER THAN USUALLY ALLOWED. THE PANZER TROOPS WORE THE BLACK LEATHER UNIFORMS USUALLY RESERVED FOR U-BOAT CREWS. AS WELL AS UNIT INSIGNIA, THEY PAINTED THE NAMES OF THEIR GIRLFRIENDS ON THE SIDES OF THEIR TANKS.

COMMANDING THE HJ WAS 34-YEAR-OLD GEN. KURT MEYER, ALREADY KNOWN TO THE GERMAN PUBLIC AS "PANZERMEYER." MEYER WAS A BATTLE-HARDENED, COMMITTED NAZI, BUT HE WAS ALSO A COURAGEOUS, CHARISMATIC LEADER. HE WAS IDEALIZED BY HIS MEN. IT WASN'T UNUSUAL FOR HIM TO PUT HIS LIFE ON THE LINE TO SAVE A WOUNDED PRIVATE. HE WAS FREQUENTLY SEEN NEAR THE FRONT LINES MAKING A PERSONAL RECON ON HIS MOTORCYCLE.

MEYER MADE HIS HEADQUARTERS IN THE ARDENNE ABBEY, WHICH PROVIDED GOOD PROTECTION AND EXCELLENT OBSERVATION ALL THE WAY TO THE ENGLISH CHANNEL.

IT WAS IN THE SHADOWS OF THE ABBEY THAT THE HJ DIVISION COMMITTED SOME OF THE OFFENSES THAT THEY ARE MOST REMEMBERED FOR: THE KILLING OF SEVERAL GROUPS OF CANADIAN PRISONERS, POSSIBLY UNDER THE DIRECT ORDERS OF PANZERMEYER.

ON JUNE 25, 3 BATTLESHIPS, 4 CRUISERS, AND 11 DESTROYERS BEGAN TO BOMBARD THE GERMAN LINES IN PREPARATION FOR OPERATION EPSON. THE BRITISH AND CANADIANS OUTNUMBERED THE GERMANS IN TANKS NEARLY 3-TO-1, IN ARTILLERY 11-TO-1, AND IN INFANTRY 4-TO-1. ON THE FIRST DAY, THE BRITISH 49TH DIVISION ATTACKED, EARNING THEMSELVES THE NICKNAME "THE BUTCHER BEARS."

ON THE SECOND DAY OF THE OFFENSIVE, THE 15TH SCOTTISH DIVISION ADVANCED THROUGH THE SHATTERED CORN, THEIR PIPERS PLAYING "COCK O' THE NORTH" AND "BLUE BONNETS OVER THE BORDER" JUST AS THEIR FATHERS DID A GENERATION EARLIER.

THE YOUNG MEN OF THE HJ OPENED FIRE ON THEM FROM THEIR WELL-CONCEALED POSITIONS. THE SCOTS WERE CUT DOWN, JUST AS THEIR FATHERS WERE A GENERATION EARLIER. IN 4 DAYS, THEIR DIVISION WOULD BE CUT IN HALF.

BY JUNE 27, THE SCOTS HAD GAINED A GREAT DEAL OF GROUND. THEY MANAGED TO CAPTURE A BRIDGE OVER THE ORNE AT TOURMANVILLE.

THE GERMANS WERE NOT ABOUT TO LET THEM KEEP IT.

ON JUNE 29, THE GERMANS THREW THEIR ARMORED WEIGHT AGAINST WHAT WAS NOW BEING CALLED THE "SCOTTISH CORRIDOR." ELEMENTS OF THE PANZER LEHR, 9TH SS, AND 10TH SS PANZER DIVISION SLAMMED INTO WHAT WAS MOSTLY INFANTRY. EVEN PORTIONS OF THE NEWLY ARRIVED 2ND SS AND 1ST SS PANZER (SISTER UNIT OF THE HJ) DIVISIONS WERE THROWN IN. THE SCOTS DUG IN, MUDDLED, WEARISOME, AND TERRIFIED, AND TAUGHT THE GERMANS THE TRUE MEANING OF THE "THIN RED LINE."

IN THIS FIGHT, NO GROUP OF SOLDIERS STOOD SO EXPOSED AS THE 2ND ARGYLL AND SUTHERLAND HIGHLANDERS. ARMED WITH NOTHING BIGGER THAN 6-POUNDERS AND PIAT ANTI-TANK GUNS, THEY FACED THE PANZERS AND MARK IVS AND STOPPED THEM IN THEIR TRACKS.

JULY 4, 5, 6, 7... THE HJ FOUGHT A SEESAW BATTLE WITH THE CANADIAN 3RD DIVISION OVER THE CONTROL OF CARPIQUET.

THIS FIGHT WAS BRUTAL BEYOND WORDS. WOULD YOU BELIEVE IT?! ONE DAY THE VETERANS WOULD MEET AND DISCUSS THESE ACTIONS OVER BEER IN THEIR OLD AGE.

JULY 8. OPERATION CHARWOOD. 450 ROYAL AIR FORCE HEAVY BOMBERS PULVERIZED CAEN. THE SMOKE AND DUST THROWN UP BY THE BOMBARDMENT BLOCKED OUT THE SUN.

WHEN THE ATTACK CAME THE NEXT DAY, KURT MEYER KNEW IT WAS USELESS. HIS YOUNG PANZERGRENADIERS DENIED THE BRITISH ANOTHER CROSSING OF THE ORNE...

...BUT HE KNEW THEIR LOSSES HAD BEEN TOO GREAT TO HOLD ON ANY LONGER. HE WITHDREW HIS FORCES TO THE SOUTH BANK OF THE RIVER. 2 DAYS LATER, THEY WERE PULLED BACK FARTHER FOR A VERY SHORT REST.

CAEN HAD BEEN THE BRITISH 2ND ARMY'S D-DAY OBJECTIVE. IT DID NOT FALL UNTIL 1 MONTH AND 3 DAYS LATER. THE BRITISH AND CANADIANS FOUND CAEN A DEAD CITY. THE AIR BOMBARDMENT HAD BEEN FUTILE, CAUSING SO MUCH RUBBLE THAT VEHICLES COULD NOT MOVE BEYOND TO ATTACK THE GERMANS ON THE OTHER SIDE. THOUSANDS OF CIVILIANS LAY DEAD AMONG THE SHATTERED BUILDINGS. THOSE WHO WERE STILL ALIVE STOOD AROUND AND GAZED AT THE CONQUERORS WITHOUT EMOTION. EVERYONE KNEW THE TRUTH, FROM GENERAL TO PRIVATE: THIS WAS LIBERATION AT A FRIGHTFUL PRICE.

NORMANDY
CHAPTER NINE
THE CAPITAL OF RUINS

FOR SOME TIME, MONTGOMERY HAD BEEN FORMULATING AND DISCUSSING A PLAN TO BREAK OUT OF THE BEACHHEAD AREA. HE SUGGESTED THAT THE MAJORITY OF THE GERMAN PANZER DIVISIONS COULD BE HELD IN PLACE BY THE BRITISH AND CANADIANS IN FRONT OF CAEN.

MEANWHILE, THE AMERICAN 1ST ARMY, AFTER A MASSIVE "CARPET BOMBING" OF THE GERMAN LINES, WOULD ATTACK SOUTH INTO THE OPEN COUNTRY BEYOND ST.-LÔ. OMAR BRADLEY WAS BEGINNING TO WARM TO THE PLAN, BUT THERE WERE SEVERAL PROBLEMS.

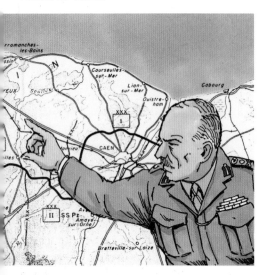

THE PLAN WOULD HAVE TO BE ACTED ON QUICKLY. THE REASON WAS THAT THE GERMANS, HAVING FINALLY RECEIVED SEVERAL FRESH UNITS TO THE CAEN AREA, WERE NOW SHIFTING PANZER UNITS TO THE AMERICAN FRONT. THE PANZER LEHR DIVISION HAD ATTACKED THE U.S. 9TH INFANTRY DIVISION AT ST.-JEAN-DE-DAYE. THE ASSAULT HAD INFLICTED HEAVY CASUALTIES AND MADE GAINS BUT WAS FINALLY PUSHED BACK.

ON THE BRIGHTER SIDE, THE AMERICANS WERE FINALLY ABLE TO FIND A WAY TO DEAL WITH THE NORMAN HEDGEROWS. BRADLEY PERSONALLY INSPECTED A DEVICE DESIGNED BY SGT. CURTIS CULIN OF THE 79 INFANTRY DIVISION. CULIN CALLED IT A "HEDGEROW CUTTER." IT WAS MADE FROM GERMAN STEEL BEACH OBSTACLES TAKEN OFF THE INVASION BEACHES. WELDED TO THE FRONT OF A TANK, THEY WOULD ALLOW THE VEHICLE TO PLOW THROUGH THE SOIL AND GROWTH, OPENING THE WAY FOR THE INFANTRY. IT WAS SIMPLE BUT BRILLIANT.

BRADLEY BEGAN FORMULATING THE BREAKOUT, TO BE CALLED OPERATION COBRA. IN THE MEANTIME, ST.-LÔ HAD TO BE TAKEN.

AS IT HAD ORIGINALLY BEEN INTENDED, THE JOB WOULD BE PERFORMED BY THE 29TH DIVISION, WHICH HAD SUFFERED CONSTANTLY SINCE ITS LANDING ON OMAHA BEACH 35 DAYS EARLIER.

THE ATTACK WOULD BEGIN AT 0600 ON JULY 11. THE 35TH DIVISION WOULD BE ON THEIR RIGHT, AND THE 2ND DIVISION ON THEIR LEFT. IT WAS LESS THAN A MILE TO ST.-LÔ, BUT THEY ALL KNEW THAT THE GERMANS WOULD FIGHT FOR EVERY YARD.

THE GERMANS HAD NO INTENTION OF LETTING THE AMERICAN PLANS GO AS SCHEDULED. AT 0130 ON THE MORNING BEFORE THE ATTACK, GERMAN PARATROOPERS ASSAULTED THE CENTER OF THE 29TH'S LINE. THE FIGHT DETERIORATED INTO A WILD MELEE. RADIO CONTACT BETWEEN UNITS MYSTERIOUSLY CEASED. SCREAMS AND YELLS AND FIRING CAME FROM EVERY DIRECTION.

AS THE FIRST RAYS OF DAWN APPEARED IN THE EASTERN SKIES, THE GERMANS BEGAN TO WITHDRAW TO THEIR OWN LINES.

THE MEN OF THE 29TH HAD MAINTAINED THEIR LINE, AND THEIR OWN ATTACK WOULD GO ON AS SCHEDULED.

AT 0500, THE DIVISION'S ARTILLERY OPENED UP WITH A FURIOUS BARRAGE.

AT 0600, THE ATTACK BEGAN RIGHT ON SCHEDULE. THE AXIS OF THE ATTACK WAS CENTERED AROUND THE 116TH INFANTRY REGIMENT. USING TANKS FITTED WITH CULIN HEDGEROW CUTTERS, THEY BUSTED THE GERMAN FRONT LINE WIDE OPEN.

THE 116TH-ASSIGNED AREA RAN ALONG A COUNTRY ROAD THE LENGTH OF A RIDGE THAT LED DIRECTLY TO ST.-LÔ. IT WAS CALLED MARTINVILLE RIDGE.

OF COURSE, ON THE RIDGE, FIGHTING IN THE HEDGEROWS, IT DIDN'T LOOK LIKE A RIDGE AT ALL, BUT JUST LIKE ANOTHER PART OF THE ENDLESS LANDSCAPE.

MAJOR TOM HOWIE COMMANDED ONE OF THE 116TH'S BATTALIONS. HE WAS KIND AND WELL MANNERED. HE WAS ONE OF THE MOST-LIKED OFFICERS IN THE DIVISION. HE HAD BEEN A TEACHER OF ENGLISH LITERATURE AND A FOOTBALL COACH. HE WOULD BECOME A SYMBOL OF THE 29TH DIVISION'S ATTACK ON GERMAN-HELD ST.-LÔ.

FINALLY, ON THE MORNING OF JULY 18, THE 29TH DIVISION ENTERED ST.-LÔ. THE CITY WAS IN SUCH A STATE OF DEVASTATION THAT ONE G.I. SAID, "WE SURE LIBERATED THE HELL OUT OF THIS PLACE." AFTER THE WAR, THE FRENCH NICKNAMED IT "THE CAPITAL OF RUINS."

MAJOR TOM HOWIE ENTERED ST.-LÔ TOO, ON THE BACK OF A JEEP, COVERED WITH AN OLIVE DRAB G.I. BLANKET.

HIS BODY WAS PLACED ON TOP OF A HUGE PILE OF RUBBLE WHICH HAD ONCE BEEN THE WALL OF THE SAINTE-CROIX CHURCH AND DRAPED WITH THE AMERICAN FLAG. HIS PICTURE APPEARED IN *LIFE* MAGAZINE WITH THE SIMPLE CAPTION "THE MAJOR OF ST.-LÔ."

THE 29TH DIVISION HAD GONE THROUGH 43 DAYS OF GRULING COMBAT. NOT A SINGLE BATTALION COULD MUSTER MORE THAN A COMPANY OF MEN. AFTER THE FALL OF ST.-LÔ, THEY WERE RELIEVED BY THE 35TH DIVISION AND WENT INTO A PERIOD OF WELL-DESERVED REST AND REBUILDING. BUT THEY STILL HAD A LOT OF WAR AHEAD OF THEM.

BLOOD & THUNDER

MONDAY, JULY 17. HAVING SUSPECTED THAT THE BRITISH WERE GOING TO MOUNT A NEW OFFENSIVE, FIELD MARSHAL ROMMEL WENT ON AN INSPECTION OF THE DEFENSES AROUND CAEN AND THE ORNE RIVER.

IN THE LATE AFTERNOON, HIS CAR WAS SPOTTED BY BRITISH PLANES. ONE FIGHTER SWOOPED IN SO QUICKLY THAT ROMMEL'S DRIVER WAS UNABLE TO FIND COVER IN TIME. THE DRIVER WAS KILLED AND ROMMEL BADLY WOUNDED. HE WAS REPLACED BY FIELD MARSHAL GÜNTHER VON KLUGE.

THE GERMANS STILL HELD THE INDUSTRIAL SOUTHERN HALF OF CAEN, WHICH SITS ON THE SOUTHERN BANKS OF THE ORNE.

THOUSANDS OF CIVILIANS LAY HIDDEN IN THE RUBBLE, HAVING NOWHERE ELSE TO GO. HUNDREDS HAD BEEN KILLED IN THE FIGHTING, BUT THE WORST LAY AHEAD.

AT 0530 ON TUESDAY, JULY 18, 1,000 BRITISH LANCASTERS AND HALIFAX BOMBERS BEGAN AN AIR ASSAULT ON CAEN AND A CORRIDOR OF COUNTRYSIDE BEYOND IT. 571 U.S. HEAVY BOMBERS CAME RIGHT BEHIND THEM, FOLLOWED BY 482 MEDIUM BOMBERS AND 300 FIGHTERS, DROPPING MORE THAN 7,000 TONS OF BOMBS IN ALL.

THE EXPLODING BOMBS THREW TONS OF DIRT INTO THE AIR, TURNING DAY INTO NIGHT. TREES WERE UPROOTED. TIGER TANKS WERE THROWN AROUND LIKE TOYS.

BUTTONED UP IN THEIR PANZERS, THE CREWS WERE RATTLED AROUND LIKE DICE IN A TIN CUP. SOME MEN WENT INSANE. A FEW COMMITTED SUICIDE.

BUT SOME UNITS WENT UNTOUCHED. THE 88MM GUNS ALONG THE TOP OF BOURGUÉBUS RIDGE WERE MISSED ALL TOGETHER.

AFTER THE PLANES HAD LEFT, A CREEPING BARRAGE BEGAN TO MOVE ACROSS THE LANDSCAPE. FROM BEHIND IT CAME THE TANKS OF 3 BRITISH ARMORED DIVISIONS. THEY CAME IN SLOWLY, MOVING IN TIGHT FORMATION, 32 IN A ROW. IT WAS A VERY IMPRESSIVE SIGHT, BUT SOMETHING WAS WRONG. THERE WAS NO INFANTRY WITH THEM. NO INFANTRY TO CLEAR OUT HIDDEN POCKETS OF RESISTANCE AND SCATTERED ANTI-TANK WEAPONS. MAYBE THE BRITISH HOPED NO ONE WOULD NOTICE. BUT SOMEONE WOULD.

THE MAN TO NOTICE WAS COL. HANS VON LUCK OF THE 21ST PANZER DIVISION. JUST BACK FROM LEAVE IN PARIS AND STILL IN HIS BEST DRESS UNIFORM, HE DASHED AROUND THE BATTLEFIELD, ORGANIZING THE DEPLOYMENT WITH ANYONE HE COULD FIND.

HE FOUND A LUFTWAFFE 88MM BATTERY WHOSE COMMANDER WAS RELUCTANT TO CONVERT HIS GUNS FROM AN ANTI-AIRCRAFT TO ANTI-TANK ROLL. VON LUCK QUICKLY CONVINCED HIM TO HIS WAY OF THINKING WITH A PISTOL AT THE MAN'S HEAD.

MEANWHILE, THE BRITISH FIFE AND FORFAR YEOMANRY WERE NEARING THE FORTIFIED VILLAGE OF CAGNY, WHEN THE GERMAN ANTI-TANK GUNS OPENED UP.

IN WHAT SEEMED A MATTER OF SECONDS, 12 TANKS WERE HIT AND BURNING. TO THEIR REAR, THE TANKS OF THE 23RD HUSSARS WERE BROUGHT TO A HALT BY THE SIGHT OF SO MANY VEHICLES SIMULTANEOUSLY BURSTING INTO FLAMES. THE SURVIVING MARK IV TANKS OF THE 21ST PANZER DIVISION BEGAN TO SHAKE OFF THE SHOCK OF THE BOMBARDMENT AND MOVE INTO ACTION.

THE MARK IV TANKS, OUTNUMBERED AND STILL
HALF CRIPPLED FROM THE BOMBARDMENT, WERE
QUICKLY DONE IN.

THE MOST FORMIDABLE THREAT CAME AT
MIDDAY FROM THE 503RD HEAVY TANK
BATTALION.

ARMED WITH TIGER TANKS, AND EVEN A FEW BRAND-NEW KING TIGERS, THE 503RD BEGAN TO
CHEW UP THE SHERMANS OF THE GUARD ARMORED DIVISION.

THE FIGHT SOON BECAME A CLOSE-RANGE SLUGFEST WITH TANKS CHARGING AND RAMMING
EACH OTHER.

ANOTHER MAJOR THORN IN THE BRITISH SIDE WAS THE 200TH ASSAULT GUN BATTALION. PART OF
VON LUCK'S BATTLE GROUP, THE 200TH'S 18 105MM GUNS MANAGED TO DO GREAT DAMAGE TO
THE 3RD ROYAL TANK REGIMENT.

THAT NIGHT, AT THE ORNE RIVER BRIDGE, A HUGE TRAFFIC JAM DEVELOPED. THIS DELAYED SUPPLIES OF FUEL AND AMMUNITION FROM REACHING THE BRITISH TANKS UP AHEAD.

THE GERMAN LUFTWAFFE, WHICH HAD BEEN MOSTLY ABSENT THAT SUMMER, CHOSE THAT MOMENT TO APPEAR. THEY INFLICTED HEAVY CASUALTIES ON THE BRITISH SUPPLY TRIPS.

EARLY THE NEXT MORNING, 46 PANZERS MOVED CAUTIOUSLY FROM ONE PATCH OF COVER TO THE OTHER. THEY WERE MOVING TOWARD THE HIGH GROUND ON THE WESTERN EDGE OF THE "ARMORED CORRIDOR" OF THE BRITISH ADVANCE.

THESE TANKS BELONGED TO JOCHEN PEIPER'S 1ST PANZER REGIMENT OF THE 1ST SS PANZER DIVISION, WHICH HAD ARRIVED A WEEK EARLIER.

BY EARLY AFTERNOON, PEIPER'S PANZERS HAD ESTABLISHED THEMSELVES ON THE HIGH GROUND. THEY HAD THE ADVANTAGE OF A NETWORK OF SUNKEN ROADS THAT PROVIDED PERFECT "HULL-DOWN" POSITIONS—THAT IS, POSITIONS WHERE THE TANK'S HULL IS BEHIND EARTH WITH ONLY THE TURRET SHOWING. PATCHES OF TREES AND SMALL VILLAGES ALSO DOTTED THE RIDGE, GIVING SHELTER FROM ROVING FIGHTER BOMBERS THAT MIGHT APPEAR.

WHEN THE BRITISH TANKS BEGAN TO ROLL, THE GERMANS WERE READY FOR THEM. THE CLASH LATER REMINDED SOME OF THE OLD QUOTE OF THE DUKE OF WELLINGTON AT WATERLOO: "THEY CAME IN THE SAME OLD WAY...

"...AND WE STOPPED THEM IN THE SAME OLD WAY."

CROMWELL TANKS OF THE NORTHHAMPTONSHIRE YEOMANRY MADE ONE LAST ATTEMPT AT BOURGUÉBUS RIDGE. THEY LEFT 16 BURNING TANKS FOR THE TROUBLE.

THAT NIGHT IT RAINED, BRINGING OPERATION GOODWOOD TO A MUDDY HALT. MORE THAN 400 BRITISH TANKS LAY CHARRED ACROSS THE LANDSCAPE SOUTH OF CAEN, AND A BREAKTHROUGH HAD NOT BEEN ACHIEVED.

YET MONTGOMERY VOICED SATISFACTION THAT THE REST OF CAEN HAD BEEN CAPTURED. THE OFFENSIVE HAD STILL HELD MOST OF THE GERMAN ARMORED FORCES IN FRONT OF THE BRITISH AND CANADIANS. AND THEY HAD DESTROYED MORE THAN 100 GERMAN TANKS IN THE FIGHT.

OTHERS WERE NOT AS HAPPY. AIR MARSHAL TEDDER WANTED MONTGOMERY RELIEVED. EISENHOWER WAS FURIOUS. GOODWOOD HAD ONLY ADVANCED 7 MILES. HE TOLD MONTGOMERY THAT THE AIR FORCE COULD NOT AFFORD TO DROP 1,000 TONS OF BOMBS FOR EACH MILE OF ADVANCE.

THINGS WERE ALSO HAPPENING ON THE OTHER SIDE OF THE LINES. ON JULY 20, A GROUP OF HITLER'S GENERALS TRIED TO KILL HIM! THE NEWS, WHEN IT REACHED THE FRONT, WAS MET WITH MIXED RESPONSES. THE YOUNG GRENADIERS OF THE HITLERJÜGEND WERE FURIOUS! OTHER GERMAN SOLDIERS KEPT THEIR OPINIONS TO THEMSELVES.

NORMANDY
CHAPTER ELEVEN
THE COBRA STRIKES!

BY LATE JULY, THE ALLIED ARMIES HAD GROWN AND SUBDIVIDED AND SUBDIVIDED AGAIN. THE WESTERN FORCES BECAME THE 12TH ARMY GROUP UNDER BRADLEY. THIS INCLUDED THE U.S. 1ST ARMY UNDER GEN. COURTNEY HODGES AND ALSO INCLUDED ELEMENTS THAT WOULD SOON BE THE U.S. 3RD ARMY UNDER GEORGE PATTON. IN THE EASTERN SECTOR AROUND CAEN WAS THE 21ST ARMY GROUP UNDER MONTGOMERY. THIS INCLUDED THE BRITISH 2ND ARMY UNDER GEN. MILES DEMPSEY AND THE CANADIAN 1ST ARMY UNDER GEN. HENRY D. G. CRERAR.

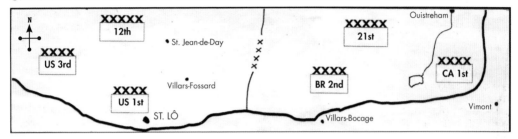

ON THE MORNING OF JULY 25, THE G.I.S OF THE U.S. 1ST ARMY TURNED THEIR EARS TOWARD A DEEP DRONING SOUND FROM THE NORTH. IT WAS THE SOUND OF 1,500 B-17 AND B-24S CARRYING 3,300 TONS OF BOMBS FOR THE GERMANS FACING THE AMERICAN LINES.

BEHIND THEM CAME 400 MEDIUM BOMBERS CARRYING 650 TONS OF BOMBS AND BEHIND THEM CAME 550 FIGHTER BOMBERS CARRYING 200 TONS OF HIGH EXPLOSIVES.

IN ADDITION THERE WOULD BE 125,000 ROUNDS OF ARTILLERY.

THE FIRST BOMBS BEGAN TO FALL, CAUSING HUGE CLOUDS OF DUST TO RISE IN THE SKY.

A LIGHT BREEZE CAUSED THIS DUST TO BLOW BACK OVER THE AMERICAN LINES. THIS INTERFERED WITH THE FOLLOWING WAVES OF BOMBERS SEEING THEIR TARGETS CLEARLY.

EXPLODING BOMBS WERE EASING BACK TOWARD THE AMERICAN LINES. THEY LANDED IN THE MIDST OF THE U.S. 30TH DIVISION. MEN RAN FOR THEIR FOXHOLES OR FOR WHATEVER COVER THEY COULD FIND. UNFORTUNATELY, THE BOMBS DIDN'T KNOW THE DIFFERENCE BETWEEN GERMANS AND AMERICANS. THEY PULVERIZED BOTH WITHOUT DISCRIMINATION.

111 MEN WERE KILLED AND 490 WOUNDED. AMONG THE DEAD WAS LT. GEN. LESLEY MCNAIR, THE HIGHEST-RANKING AMERICAN TO DIE IN WORLD WAR II.

MANY COMMANDERS FELT THAT THIS DEBACLE SHOULD DELAY THE ADVANCE, BUT VII CORPS COMMANDER GEN. LAWTON COLLINS SAID, "NO! PUSH OFF! JUMP OFF IMMEDIATELY! THERE WAS NO TIME TO WASTE! HIT THE GERMANS NOW!"

SHAKING OFF THE SHOCK, THE U.S. 9TH, 4TH, AND 30TH DIVISIONS MOVED FORWARD. WOULD IT BE THE SAME OLD STORY WITH THE GERMANS WAITING BEHIND EVERY HEDGEROW?

THERE WERE NO HEDGEROWS. BEFORE THE AMERICANS WAS A MOON-LIKE LANDSCAPE. TANKS HAD BEEN OVERTURNED AND SHATTERED LIKE EGGS. GERMAN SOLDIERS HAD BEEN BLOWN TO BITS OR EVEN VAPORIZED. THOSE WHO SURVIVED WERE FREQUENTLY DEAF OR INSANE. 1,000 MEN OF THE PANZER LEHR DIVISION HAD SIMPLY DISAPPEARED.

BUT THOSE GERMANS WHO DID SURVIVE BEGAN TO RECOVER AND THEN BEGAN TO FIGHT!

AS THE DAY WORE ON, THE AMERICAN ADVANCE BEGAN TO SLOW AND GENERAL COLLINS WORRIED. WOULD THE BREAKTHROUGH BE STOPPED?

COLLINS DECIDED TO GAMBLE. ON THE MORNING OF JULY 26, HE COMMITTED HIS ARMOR ELEMENTS OF THE U.S. 2ND AND 3RD ARMORED DIVISIONS, ALONG WITH THE 1ST DIVISION, WHICH HAD BEEN MOTORIZED FOR THE OCCASION. THERE WAS HARD FIGHTING FOR THE REST OF THE DAY AND INTO THE NEXT MORNING.

AS THE 3RD ARMORED DIVISION ADVANCED, THEY CAME UP AGAINST A LONE PANTHER TANK OF THE 2ND SS PANZER DIVISION.

THE COMMANDER OF THIS PANTHER WAS ERNST BARKMANN, WHO HAD ALREADY BUILT A TOUGH REPUTATION WITH THE "DAS REICH" DIVISION. PARKED UNDER A HUGE OAK TREE SO AS TO HIDE FROM FIGHTER-BOMBERS FLYING OVERHEAD, BARKMANN'S TANK KNOCKED OUT 9 SHERMAN TANKS AND SEVERAL GAS TANKER TRUCKS WITH THEM.

PLANES AND TANKS FINALLY FORCED BARKMANN TO RETREAT, BUT NOT BEFORE HE HAD LOST A TRACK AND ALMOST RUN OUT OF AMMUNITION.

THE AMERICANS HAD THEIR "TANK ACES," TOO. IN THE 3RD ARMORED DIVISION WAS TEXAN SGT. LAFAYETTE POOL. IN 83 DAYS OF COMBAT, POOL AND HIS TANK CREW DESTROYED 258 ARMORED VEHICLES. POOL'S TRADEMARK WAS WEARING COWBOY BOOTS IN BATTLE. HE KEPT HIS TANK IN THE ADVANCE OF THE 3RD ARMORED UNTIL HE WAS WOUNDED AND LOST A LEG IN BELGIUM ON SEPTEMBER 8.

MEN LIKE BARKMANN COULD NOT BE EVERYWHERE ON THE GERMAN FRONT. THE LINE BEGAN TO CRACK AND THE CONSTANT PRESENCE OF ALLIED AIR SUPERIORITY EVEN MADE RETREAT DANGEROUS. ON JULY 29, A GERMAN CONVOY WAS SPOTTED NEAR RONCEY. FOR 6 HOURS, BRITISH AND AMERICAN PLANES TORE INTO THE TRAFFIC JAM, DESTROYING MORE THAN 100 TANKS AND OVER 250 OTHER VEHICLES.

TO THE EAST, NEAR THE ATLANTIC COAST, THE VIII CORPS, WHICH INCLUDED THE U.S. 4TH AND 6TH ARMORED DIVISIONS, BEGAN MOVING SOUTH. THIS UNIT WAS THE FIRST ELEMENT OF THE 3RD ARMY AND WAS COMMANDED BY GEORGE PATTON.

THE TANKERS OF THE VIII CORPS WERE VERY RESPONSIVE TO PATTON'S STYLE OF WARFARE. THEY MOVED FAST, KNIFING THROUGH LIGHT RESISTANCE, LEAVING LITTLE POCKETS OF RESISTANCE BEHIND TO BE HANDLED BY THE INFANTRY. BY AUGUST 3, THEY WERE NEARING NANTES, WHICH WOULD CUT OFF ALL GERMAN TROOPS IN BRITTANY.

VON KLUGE, IN HIS 7TH ARMY COMMAND POST IN LE MANS, WAS IN DESPAIR. "THE WHOLE WESTERN FRONT HAS BEEN RIPPED WIDE OPEN," HE RADIOED HITLER. "THE LEFT FLANK HAS COLLAPSED." HE ASKED PERMISSION TO WITHDRAW TO THE SEINE.

HITLER WOULD NOT GIVE VON KLUGE PERMISSION TO WITHDRAW. HE ORDERED HIM TO ATTACK! HE WANTED THE ATTACK TO GO AGAINST THE U.S. 3RD ARMY'S FLANK, CUTTING THEM OFF FROM THEIR SUPPLIES AND THE REST OF THEIR FORCES.

ON THE SAME DAY, TROOPS OF THE U.S. 30TH DIVISION LIBERATED THE SMALL CITY OF MORTAIN. THE POPULATION THERE HAD BEEN REMARKABLY FORTUNATE, SUFFERING ALMOST NO DAMAGE AS THE AMERICANS CAME IN AND THE GERMANS MOVED OUT. THE TOWN FATHERS OFFERED THANKS TO GOD FOR SPARING THEIR HOMES THE DESTRUCTION THAT AFFECTED NEARBY TOWNS LIKE VIRE, TESSY, AND ST.-LÔ.

HERE, CELEBRATION WAS PREMATURE...

NORMANDY
CHAPTER TWELVE
"COME AND GET US!"

EARLY IN THE WAR BRITISH INTELLIGENCE WAS ABLE TO BREAK THE CODE USED BY THE GERMAN ENIGMA MACHINE OPERATORS. THIS EVENT, ONE OF THE MOST IMPORTANT PROJECTS OF THE ENTIRE WAR, WAS CODENAMED "ULTRA." THE PROJECT WAS SO IMPORTANT THAT THE KNOWLEDGE OF ITS EXISTENCE WAS ONLY KNOWN TO ARMY COMMANDERS AND ABOVE. THE USE OF INFORMATION RECEIVED THROUGH ULTRA WAS GUARDED CLOSELY SO THE GERMANS WOULD NEVER DISCOVER THAT THEIR CODE HAD BEEN BROKEN.

ON THE AFTERNOON OF AUGUST 6, ULTRA OPERATIVES INTERCEPTED A MESSAGE FROM GERMAN 7TH ARMY HEADQUARTERS TO THE LUFTWAFFE IN PARIS REQUESTING NIGHT FIGHTER PROTECTION FOR THE 2ND PANZER, 1ST SS, AND 2ND SS PANZER IN AN ATTACK THROUGH MORTAIN TO ST.-HILAIRE.

PATTON THOUGHT IT WAS A BLUFF, BUT JUST IN CASE HE STOPPED THE U.S. 80TH AND 35TH DIVISION, ALONG WITH THE NEWLY ACTIVATED FRENCH 2ND ARMORED DIVISION IN THE VICINITY OF ST.-HILAIRE. BRADLEY CONTACTED THE ALLIED AIR FORCES FOR ALL-OUT SUPPORT AS SOON AS DAWN BROKE ON AUGUST 7.

THE 30TH DIVISION WAS NOTIFIED: "HOLD MORTAIN AT ALL COST!"

THE EARLY MORNING HOURS OF AUGUST 7 WERE SHROUDED IN AN IMPENETRABLE FOG THAT WAS ILLUMINATED BY THE FULL MOON. IN THIS EERIE LIGHT, PANZERGRENADIERS OF THE 2ND SS PANZER DIVISION HIT THE OUTPOST OF THE U.S. 30TH DIVISION. THEY QUICKLY PUSHED THE AMERICANS BACK INTO THE TOWN OF MORTAIN.

THE G.I.S, NOT AS EXPERIENCED IN NIGHT FIGHTING AS THE GERMANS, QUICKLY GAVE GROUND. BUT THIS WAS NOT AN INEXPERIENCED DIVISION. PLATOON AND SQUAD LEADERS SOON TOOK CONTROL AND THE LINE HELD.

THE FIGHTING WAS NOISY AND DEADLY WITH BOTH SIDES USING EVERY WEAPON THEY HAD. MOST OF THE TOWN CAUGHT FIRE.

AT DAWN, THE MEN OF THE 30TH BEGAN TO FEEL THE FULL WEIGHT OF THE GERMAN ASSAULT AS PANZERS BEGAN TO ROLL TOWARD THEM.

HOWEVER, THE MEN OF THE 30TH WERE MORE PREPARED THAN THE GERMANS EXPECTED. A GROUP OF CAREFULLY PLACED 3-INCH ANTI-TANKS GUNS COMMANDED BY LT. TOM SPRINGFIELD...

...STOPPED THE GERMANS AT EVERY TURN. THE STREETS OF MORTAIN, AND ROADS AROUND IT, WERE SOON LITTERED WITH THE BURNING WRECKS OF GERMAN ARMORED VEHICLES.

BUT FLESH AND BONE CANNOT HOLD OUT FOREVER AGAINST FIRE AND STEEL. ONE AMERICAN BATTALION FOUND ITSELF BACKING ONTO A RISE KNOWN AS HILL 314.

FROM THERE THEY WERE CUT OFF FROM SUPPLIES OF FOOD, WATER, AND AMMO. BUT AS LONG AS THEY HAD AMPLE SUPPLIES WITH THEM THEM, THEY COULD SHOOT ANY GERMAN TRYING TO REACH THEM. THEY SOON DISCOVERED THAT THEIR DEADLIEST WEAPON WAS NOT RIFLES OR GRENADES.

IT WAS A RADIO! WITH THEM ON THE HILL WERE FORWARD ARTILLERY OBSERVERS. FROM THEIR LOFTY PERCH, THESE SOLDIERS COULD CALL IN ACCURATE FIRE FROM FRIENDLY CANNONS WITHIN RANGE.

THIS ARTILLERY FIRE MADE IT VERY DIFFICULT FOR THE GERMANS BELOW TO ORGANIZE AN EFFECTIVE ASSAULT ON THE HILL.

MEANWHILE, A FARMER AND HIS WIFE WHO LIVED ON THE HILL HELPED BY SHARING THEIR FEW CHICKENS, POTATOES, AND CABBAGE WITH THE AMERICANS.

BUT AS DAYS PASSED THE SITUATION BECAME MORE DESPERATE. FOOD AND WATER WAS RUNNING LOW. THE MOST IMPORTANT THING WAS THAT THE RADIO BATTERIES WERE GETTING WEAK.

OMAR BRADLEY PICKED A SIZABLE FORCE TO AID THE BELEAGURED 30TH DIVISION. AFTER CONSIDERABLE THOUGHT, HE EXPLORED ANOTHER OPTION. PATTON'S FORCES WERE MAKING GOOD PROGRESS SOUTHWARD. WHAT IF THE 30TH WAS LEFT ALONE AT MORTAIN FOR THE TIME BEING, UNAIDED AND APPARENTLY ON THE VERGE OF COLLAPSE? THIS WOULD ENCOURAGE THE GERMANS TO KEEP PRESSING WESTWARD. WITH THE BULK OF THE PANZER FORCES SO OCCUPIED, PATTON'S FORCES COULD SWEEP TO THE EAST TOWARD LE MANS ON THE SARTHE RIVER. THEY WOULD THEN SWEEP NORTH. IF THE BRITISH AND CANADIANS COULD BREAK THROUGH TO THE SOUTH, THE 2 FORCES COULD MEET IN THE VICINITY OF FALAISE AND ARGENTAN. THIS COULD COMPLETELY ENCIRCLE 2 FULL GERMAN ARMIES, THE 5TH PANZER ARMY AND THE 7TH ARMY.

IT WAS A REMARKABLE, COLD-BLOODED PLAN. INSTEAD OF PROVIDING RELIEF FOR THE MEN OF THE 30TH, BRADLEY WAS LEAVING THEM IN THEIR PRECARIOUS SITUATION AS BAIT FOR THE GERMANS. WHEN HE EXPLAINED THE PLAN TO EISENHOWER, HE WAS HONEST ABOUT THE RISK. IKE THOUGHT THE REWARD WAS WORTH THE GAMBLE AND HE APPROVED THE PLAN. IT IS DOUBTFUL IF EITHER GENERAL SLEPT WELL OVER THE DECISION. A GAMBLE ALWAYS LOOKS BRILLIANT IF IT SUCCEEDS.

BUT IF IT FAILS? THINGS DIDN'T LOOK GOOD FOR THE SOLDIERS ON HILL 314. IT DIDN'T HELP THAT THE SOUTHWARD PROGRESS OF THE BRITISH AND CANADIAN FORCES WAS VERY SLOW. THE YOUNG MEN OF THE 12TH SS PANZER DIVISION WERE ONCE MORE IN THE LINE AND THEY FACED THE NEWLY COMMITTED POLISH 1ST ARMORED DIVISION. IN ONE ENGAGEMENT, PANZERMEYER'S BOYS MANAGED TO KNOCK OUT 26 POLISH SHERMAN TANKS.

IT WAS A VERY COSTLY FIGHT FOR THE GERMANS TOO. NEAR THE VILLAGE OF CINTHEAUX, MICHAEL WITTMANN AND HIS CREW WERE KILLED WHEN THEIR TIGER TANK WAS DESTROYED BY A GROUP OF BRITISH FIREFLIES.

ON THE MORNING OF AUGUST 9, THE SCENE ON HILL 314 WAS GRIM. THE BODIES OF BOTH AMERICANS AND GERMANS WERE DETERIORATING QUICKLY IN THE AUGUST HEAT. SEVERAL OF THE MOST SEVERLY WOUNDED HAD DIED DURING THE NIGHT. THERE WAS NO FOOD AND ALL THE WATER THAT WAS LEFT HAD BEEN DISTRIBUTED. THE AMMUNITION SUPPLY WAS VERY LOW. MANY OF THE MEN FELT THAT THE END WAS NEAR.

LATER THAT DAY, AN SS OFFICER WALKED UP THE HILL UNDER A FLAG OF TRUCE. HE TOLD THE OFFICERS THAT HE PERSONALLY ADMIRED THE STAND THEY HAD MADE. HE ALSO POINTED OUT THAT "THE SITUATION WAS HOPELESS," AND THAT "THERE WAS NOTHING DISHONORABLE ABOUT SURRENDERING IN THESE CONDITIONS."

BEFORE THE OFFICERS COULD ANSWER, MEN IN NEARBY FOXHOLES STARTED JEERING AT THE SS OFFICER. SEVERAL SHOUTED, "DON'T SURRENDER." CAPTAIN REYNOLD ERICHSON, IN COMMAND OF THE TROOPS OF HILL 314, DECIDED HIS MEN DESERVED THE LAST WORD.

SEVERAL OF THE OTHER OFFICERS PRESENT GAVE THEIR TWO CENTS, MUCH OF WHICH IS UNPRINTABLE. LIEUTENANT RONALD WOODY CAPTURED THE SPIRIT OF THEIR ATTITUDE AS MUCH AS ANYONE: "YOU CAN GO TO HELL!" HE TOLD THE GERMAN. "IF YOU WANT US, YOU CAN COME AND GET US."

NORMANDY
CHAPTER THIRTEEN
THIRD ARMY RAMPAGE

GENERAL GEORGE SMITH PATTON'S AXIOM OF WAR WAS SIMPLE: ATTACK! KEEP MOVING! ALWAYS GO FORWARD! NEVER STOP! HE BELIEVED, QUITE FRANKLY, IN THE METHODS THAT THE GERMANS HAD PERFECTED EARLIER IN THE WAR AGAINST POLAND AND FRANCE. BLITZKRIEG. LIGHTNING WAR. THAT WAS WHAT HE WAS NOW DOING TO THE GERMANS IN NORMANDY.

ONE OF THE GREAT ADVANTAGES PATTON HAD WAS THAT HIS SUBORDINATES EITHER BELIEVED AS HE DID OR QUICKLY LEARNED HIS STYLE OF DRIVING MEN AND MACHINES.

ON THE DIVISIONAL LEVEL, THERE WAS GEN. "TIGER JACK" WOOD, WHO COMMANDED THE U.S. 4TH ARMORED DIVISION.

WITHIN WOOD'S DIVISION WAS COL. CREIGHTON ABRAMS OF THE 37TH TANK BATTALION. ABRAMS WOULD WIN 2 DISTINGUISHED SERVICE CROSSES AND GO ON TO BE THE ARMY CHIEF OF STAFF.

CORPS COMMANDERS LIKE GEROW, WALKER, AND MIDDLETON PERFECTLY COMPLEMENTED HIS HARD-DRIVING ATTITUDE.

PATTON'S MEN UNDERSTOOD HIM. THEY KNEW THAT UNDER "OLD BLOOD & GUTS" THERE WOULD BE NO HALF MEASURES. THEY ALSO KNEW THAT THE QUICKEST WAY HOME WAS TO MOVE FORWARD AND KILL THE ENEMY BEFORE HE COULD KILL YOU.

A BIG PART OF BRADLEY'S PLAN WAS FOR THE 3RD ARMY TO DRIVE EAST ACROSS THE MAYENNE RIVER AND 40 MILES FARTHER TO CAPTURE LE MANS ON THE SARTHE.

ALL THE GENERALS HAD THEIR FAVORITE FORCES THEY WOULD HAVE LIKED TO HAVE GIVEN THE ASSIGNMENT TO, BUT BECAUSE OF THE SITUATION, THIS TOUGH JOB WAS GIVEN TO 2 VERY UNRELIABLE INFANTRY DIVISIONS.

BOTH THE U.S. 79TH AND 90TH INFANTRY DIVISIONS HAD SEEN ACTION IN THE NORMANDY CAMPAIGN AND HAD PERFORMED SO POORLY THAT SEVERAL COMMANDERS HAD BEEN SACKED. NOW THEY CAME UNDER THE COMMAND OF THE NEWLY FORMED XV CORPS UNDER THE COMMAND OF GEN. WADE HAISLIP. "PUSH ALL PERSONNEL TO THE LIMIT OF HUMAN ENDURANCE," HAISLIP TOLD THE DIVISIONS' NEW COMMANDERS. "YOUR ACTIONS DURING THE NEXT FEW DAYS MIGHT BE DECISIVE FOR THE ENTIRE CAMPAIGN IN EUROPE."

AUGUST 5. FULLY MOTORIZED, THE 2 DIVISIONS CUT FORWARD, THEIR FLANKS PROTECTED BY FIGHTER-BOMBERS.

THE 90TH DIVISION TRAVELED THE 31 MILES TO THE MAYENNE RIVER ON THE EVENING OF THE FIRST DAY. THE 79TH REACHED THE RIVER JUST BEFORE MIDNIGHT. IT TOOK MOST OF THE NEXT DAY TO GET THE 2 DIVISIONS ACROSS THE MAYENNE. BY THE TIME THEY WERE READY TO MOVE, THE U.S. 5TH ARMORED DIVISION ARRIVED AND WOULD BE GUARDING THE SPEARHEAD'S SOUTHERN FLANK.

MEANWHILE, THE GERMANS WERE STILL POUNDING AWAY AT THE 30TH DIVISION AT MORTAIN. ULTRA INTERCEPTS REVEALED THAT HITLER HAD NO INTENTION OF STOPPING THE ATTACK.

HITLER WAS TOO FAR AWAY TO WITNESS THE REALITY OF THE SITUATION. HE COULDN'T SEE WHAT THE ALLIED AIR FORCES WERE DOING TO GERMAN SUPPLY UNITS TRYING TO FEED, ARM, AND FUEL THE FORCES ATTACKING MORTAIN.

FROM THE NORTH, THE CANADIANS WERE BEGINNING TO MAKE SLOW HEADWAY AGAINST THE 12TH SS. THE THING THAT BOTH THE BRITISH AND CANADIANS SORELY LACKED WAS DECENT ARMORED TROOP TRANSPORT. CANADIAN GEN. G. G. SIMONDS CAME UP WITH THE IDEA TO REMOVE THE GUNS FROM M7 SELF-PROPELLED HOWITZERS THAT THE BRITISH CALLED "PRIESTS." THESE "UNFROCKED PRIESTS" WERE ABLE TO CARRY ABOUT 10 INFANTRYMEN.

BUT PROGRESS FOR THE CANADIAN 3RD DIVISION WAS SLOW. THE TEENAGERS OF THE 12TH SS STILL STOOD IN THEIR PATH AND THEY HAD NO INTENTION OF MOVING.

ON AUGUST 9, XV CORPS REACHED LE MANS. GENERAL PATTON IMMEDIATELY BEGAN TO TURN HIS FORCES TO THE NORTH TO HEAD FOR LINK-UP WITH BRITISH AND CANADIANS.

VON KLUGE BEGAN TO UNDERSTAND THE VERY DIFFICULT SITUATION HE WAS ABOUT TO FIND HIMSELF IN. HE BEGGED HITLER TO LET HIM WITHDRAW FROM THIS SCARY POSITION.

SINCE THE ATTEMPT ON HIS LIFE IN JULY, HITLER HAD LOST A LOT OF TRUST IN HIS GENERALS. HE WAS QUICKLY LOSING HIS TRUST IN VON KLUGE.

HE REFUSED TO LET VON KLUGE WITHDRAW FROM HIS POSITION SOUTH OF CAEN. HOWEVER, HE DID ALLOW HIM TO BREAK OFF THE ATTACK ON MORTAIN ON AUGUST 11.

THE NEXT DAY, THE U.S. 35TH INFANTRY DIVISION RELIEVED THE 30TH DIVISION AT MORTAIN. HALF THE DEFENDERS OF HILL 314 WERE DEAD OR WOUNDED. THE OTHERS WERE SO EXHAUSTED THAT THEY HAD TO BE CARRIED DOWN THE HILL.

THE TOWN OF MORTAIN, WHICH HAD ONCE CELEBRATED ITS DELIVERANCE FROM THE FIGHTING, WAS NOW COMPLETELY SHATTERED.

THE MEN OF THE 30TH GOT 1 DAY'S REST, THEN WERE SENT BACK INTO COMBAT.

AS PATTON'S FORCES PUSHED NORTH AND THE BRITISH AND CANADIANS PUSHED SOUTH, THE DANGEROUS SITUATION FOR THE GERMANS BECAME CLEAR. VON KLUGE INSISTED TO HITLER THAT THE ONLY WAY TO SAVE HIS FORCES WAS TO ALLOW HIM TO WITHDRAW EAST ACROSS THE SEINE. THERE WAS ANOTHER DANGER TO THE GERMAN FORCES IN FRANCE UNBEKNOWNST TO HITLER AND VON KLUGE. IN NAPLES, ITALY, 3 TOUGH, VETERAN AMERICAN DIVISIONS, THE 3RD, 36TH, AND 45TH, WERE BOARDING SHIPS WITH THE OBJECTIVE OF AN AMPHIBIOUS LANDING IN SOUTHERN FRANCE!

BY SUNDAY, AUGUST 13, THE U.S. XV CORPS HAD TAKEN ARGENTAN. IT WAS NOW CLEAR TO ANYONE IN THE GERMAN ARMY, FROM HITLER DOWN TO THE LOWEST PRIVATE, WHAT THE SITUATION WAS. IF THEY DIDN'T QUICKLY ESCAPE TO THE EAST THEY WOULD BE TRAPPED THE WAY THEY HAD BEEN AT STALINGRAD BY THE RUSSIANS NEARLY 2 YEARS EARLIER. ONCE SURROUNDED, THE GERMANS INSIDE WOULD BE FACED WITH THE CHOICE OF SURRENDERING OR FIGHTING TO THE DEATH.

IT WAS THE RESPONSIBILITY OF THE CANADIANS TO CLOSE THE POCKET ON THE NORTHERN SIDE BY TAKING FALAISE. BUT THEIR PROGRAM WAS SLOW, LEADING TO CRITICISM BY AMERICAN COMMANDERS. PATTON WAS SO ANGERED BY THEIR SLOW ADVANCE THAT HE ASKED BRADLEY FOR PERMISSION TO PUSH ON THROUGH TO FALAISE SO HE COULD "DRIVE THE BRITISH (AND CANADIAN) INTO THE SEA" JUST LIKE AT DUNKIRK IN 1940.

BRADLEY QUICKLY SAID NO TO PATTON'S REQUEST. HE DIDN'T WANT THE ALLIED ARMIES RUNNING INTO EACH OTHER IN SUCH A DANGEROUS MANNER. HE KNEW THAT THE BRITISH AND CANADIANS WERE HAVING DIFFICULTY IN THEIR SECTORS AND THAT THEY WOULD SIMPLY NEED MORE TIME.

THE WEIGHT AND POWER OF THE ALLIED ARMIES WAS CLOSING IN ON A VERY SMALL AREA. ON AUGUST 14, THE ROYAL AIR FORCE DROPPED 4,000 TONS OF BOMBS TO AID THE CANADIAN ADVANCE OVER THE LAST 5 MILES TO FALAISE. AS IN THE PAST, THIS TACTICAL USE OF HEAVY BOMBERS WAS DANGEROUS TO BOTH SIDES. 65 CANADIAN AND POLISH TROOPS WERE KILLED AND 241 WOUNDED. PROGRESS TOWARD FALAISE WAS STILL SLOW.

ON AUGUST 15, VON KLUGE WAS TOURING AN AREA OF THE BATTLEFIELD WHEN A BRITISH FIGHTER STRAFED HIS STAFF CAR AND CAUSED HIM TO TAKE COVER IN A DITCH. MISSING FROM HEADQUARTERS UNTIL THE NEXT MORNING, HITLER FALSELY THOUGHT HE WAS NEGOTIATING WITH THE ALLIES TO SURRENDER HIS ARMY.

HITLER RELIEVED VON KLUGE OF HIS COMMAND AND HAD HIM RETURNED TO GERMANY UNDER ARREST. RATHER THAN BE FACED WITH HITLER'S INSANE CHARGES, VON KLUGE COMMITTED SUICIDE BY TAKING POTASSIUM CYANIDE.

THE CANADIAN 2ND DIVISION REACHED THE NORTHERN OUTSKIRTS OF FALAISE ON AUGUST 16 AND A BITTER BATTLE BEGAN. BY LATE IN THE DAY MOST OF THE GERMANS HAD BEEN CLEARED EXCEPT FOR ONE TROUBLESOME POCKET OF FANATICAL RESISTANCE.

60 HITLER YOUTH OF THE 12TH SS PANZER DIVISION WERE HOLDING OUT IN THE ÈCOLE SUPÈRIEURE, A CATHOLIC GIRLS' SCHOOL, AND REFUSED TO SURRENDER.

FINALLY, IN THE EARLY HOURS OF FRIDAY, AUGUST 18, CANADIAN TANKS SURROUNDED THE BUILDING AND BLASTED IT TO BITS.

SOME GERMANS WERE SEEN ESCAPING OUT THE BACK. THE REST WERE DEAD.

ON THAT SAME DAY, AMERICANS OF THE 90TH DIVISION AND POLES OF THE POLISH 1ST ARMORED DIVISION MET AT CHAMBOIS. THE FALAISE POCKET, AS IT WAS NOW BEING CALLED, HAD BEEN CLOSED. HOWEVER, THE EASTERN BOUNDARY OF THE POCKET WAS VERY POROUS. GERMAN TROOPS WERE SLIPPING AND FIGHTING THEIR WAY OUT AT MANY POINTS. HOLDING ALL THE GERMANS WITHIN THE POCKET WOULD NOT ONLY BE DIFFICULT BUT POTENTIALLY VERY DANGEROUS.

BY NOW THE POCKET WAS ONLY ABOUT 6 MILES DEEP AND 7 MILES WIDE.
WITHIN THE POCKET WAS WHAT REMAINED OF THE GERMAN 5TH PANZER
AND 7TH ARMIES. WITH VON KLUGE DISMISSED, HITLER GAVE COMMAND
OF THIS FORCE TO ONE OF HIS FAVORITES, FIELD MARSHAL WALTER
MODEL. MODEL WAS A LOYAL NAZI WHO HAD PERFORMED ADMIRABLY ON
THE RUSSIAN FRONT. HOWEVER, THE JOB OF RESCUING THE FORCES
WITHIN THE FALAISE POCKET WAS PROBABLY BEYOND ANYONE'S ABILITY.

A TREMENDOUS EFFORT WAS BEING MADE BY THE 2ND SS PANZER
CORPS TO KEEP THE ESCAPE ROUTE OPEN. THIS WAS HAMPERED BY
SPITFIRES, TYPHOONS, MUSTANGS, LIGHTNINGS, AND THUNDERBOLTS OF
THE SECOND TACTICAL AIR FORCE. THE PILOTS COULD CLEARLY SEE THE
CONSIDERABLE NUMBER OF MOTOR TRANSPORTS ON THE CONGESTED
ROADS. ONE BRITISH PILOT CALLED IT THE "BANK HOLIDAY RUSH."

THE TECHNIQUE USED IN ATTACKING THESE LONG COLUMNS WAS SIMPLE.
THE TYPHOONS WOULD BEGIN BY ACCURATELY DROPPING BOMBS ON THE
FIRST AND LAST VEHICLES, PINNING THE OTHERS ON THE ROAD. THEN
THEY WOULD COME BACK AND FIRE THEIR ROCKETS AND CANNONS.
TRUCKS CARRYING FUEL OR AMMUNITION EXPLODED DRAMATICALLY.
TANKS AND OTHER ARMORED VEHICLES WOULD TRY TO ESCAPE TO
NEIGHBORING FIELDS, BUT THEY WERE HUNTED UNMERCIFULLY BY THE
FIGHTER-BOMBERS.

WHEN THE FIGHTER-BOMBERS WERE THROUGH, THE FIGHTERS CAME IN AND THEIR CANNONS AND MACHINE GUNS CHEWED UP EVERYTHING THAT THE TYPHOONS HAD LEFT BEHIND. MUCH OF THE GERMAN ARMY'S TRANSPORT OF SUPPLIES AND ARTILLERY WERE PULLED BY HORSES. THEIR SCREAMS OF FEAR AND PAIN WERE EVERYWHERE; MEN JUMPED FROM VEHICLES AND WAGONS AND ATTEMPTED TO ESCAPE ON FOOT, BUT THE FIGHTERS WENT AFTER THE SMALL GROUPS AND EVEN INDIVIDUALS.

AIRFIELDS HAD BEEN ESTABLISHED NEARBY SO THE PLANES COULD BE QUICKLY REFUELED, REARMED, AND RESUME ATTACKING IN A MATTER OF MINUTES.

BY THE END OF FRIDAY, AUGUST 18, 1,471 SORTIES HAD BEEN FLOWN BY ALLIED PLANES. PILOTS CLAIMED 1,100 VEHICLES AND 90 TANKS.

THE POCKET RESEMBLED A GIANT WATER BOTTLE BEING SQUEEZED FROM ALL SIDES. THE GERMANS WERE DOING THEIR BEST TO BE "SPRAYED OUT OF THE EASTERN END," BUT THE ALLIES WANTED TO CAP THE BOTTLE AND KEEP THE FORCES INSIDE TO BE SQUEEZED TO DEATH OR BE FORCED TO SURRENDER. IT WOULD TAKE HARD, DETERMINED TROOPS TO CORK THE BOTTLE BECAUSE THE "WATER" INSIDE WAS "BOILING HOT."

THAT FRIDAY EVENING, 15 TANKS OF THE 19TH ARMORED RECONNOISSANCE REGIMENT OF THE CANADIAN 4TH ARMORED DIVISION ADVANCED TOWARD ST.-LAMBERT-SUR-DIVES, WHICH SAT RIGHT IN THE PATH OF THE RETREATING GERMANS. IN COMMAND WAS MAJ. D. V. CURRIE AND UNDER HIS COMMAND WERE 55 INFANTRYMEN OF THE ARGYLE AND SUTHERLAND HIGHLANDERS.

THEY REACHED THE VILLAGE JUST BEFORE DAWN ON SATURDAY AND IMMEDIATELY CAME UNDER FIRE FROM A GERMAN TIGER TANK, WHICH KNOCKED OUT THE LEAD CANADIAN SHERMAN TANK. THE TIGER WAS SOON PUT OUT OF ACTION BY CANADIAN INFANTRY.

FOR THE NEXT 3 DAYS, CURRIE AND HIS MEN FOUGHT A BITTER, BLOODY BATTLE IN AN ATTEMPT TO BLOCK THE GERMAN RETREAT. IN AN ALL-OUT EFFORT TO ESCAPE THE POCKET, GERMAN TROOPS ATTACKED THE CANADIANS IN WAVES THAT FREQUENTLY BROKE INTO HAND-TO-HAND FIGHTING. AT NIGHT, CURRIE WAS FORCED TO BACK HIS TANKS INTO A CIRCLE IN ORDER TO AVOID BEING OVERRUN.

FOR HIS BRAVE AND SKILLFUL COMMANDING OF THE DEFENSE OF ST.-LAMBERT-SUR-DIVES, MAJ. D. V. CURRIE WAS AWARDED THE VICTORIA CROSS, THE HIGHEST MILITARY DECORATION IN THE BRITISH EMPIRE.

SEVERAL MILES TO THE EAST, MEN OF THE POLISH 1ST ARMORED DIVISION TOOK A POSITION ON MONT-ORMEL, AN 800-FOOT RIDGE THAT DOMINATED THE GERMAN ESCAPE ROUTE.

MANY OF THESE POLES HAD BEEN FIGHTING THE GERMANS SINCE 1939. THEY WERE TOUGH AND VENGEFUL AND FULLY AWARE THAT THEY WOULD PROBABLY NEVER SEE POLAND AGAIN.

BECAUSE OF THE SHAPE OF THE RIDGE, THE POLES CALLED IT THE *MACZUGA* (MACE). THEY WERE CONSTANTLY ATTACKED BY GERMANS TRYING TO ESCAPE THE POCKET, BUT THEIR BIGGEST PROBLEM WAS ASSAULT FROM THE 2ND SS AND 9TH SS PANZER DIVISIONS THAT HAD BEEN ASSIGNED THE JOB OF KEEPING THE ESCAPE ROUTE OPEN.

THESE MEN HAD NO IDEA THAT IN WARSAW THE POLISH UNDERGROUND ARMY WAS BEING CRUSHED BY SS UNITS, SETTING THE STAGE FOR A SOVIET-INSTALLED GOVERNMENT TO TAKE OVER THEIR COUNTRY. BECAUSE OF THIS, THE SURVIVORS OF THE "MACE" WOULD NEVER BE ALLOWED TO RETURN HOME.

CANADIAN FORCES RELIEVED THE POLES ON THE MORNING OF AUGUST 21. THERE THEY FOUND THE BODIES OF 325 POLES WHO HAD DIED IN DEFENSE OF THE "MACE." ROYAL CANADIAN ENGINEERS BURIED THE MEN AND PLACED A SIMPLE SIGNBOARD.

BY MONDAY, THE GERMANS LEFT IN THE POCKET HAD LITTLE HOPE. MORE THAN 50,000, INCLUDING 3 GENERALS, WALKED INTO CAPTIVITY.

THE FALAISE POCKET LOOKED LIKE A SCENE FROM HELL. AN AMERICAN OFFICER REMARKED IT WAS LIKE "AN AVENGING ANGEL HAD SWEPT THE AREA BENT ON DESTROYING ALL THINGS GERMAN." GENERAL EISENHOWER SAID, "YOU COULD WALK FOR 100 YARDS ONLY STEPPING ON BODIES."

THE SMELL WAS ALSO TERRIBLE. THE PILOTS OF LOW-FLYING PLANES COULD SMELL THE STENCH OF 2,000 DEAD HORSES THAT LAY SWELLING IN THE AUGUST SUN.

THE BODIES OF MORE THAN 10,000 GERMAN SOLDIERS LAY WITHIN THE POCKET AREA. 5,000 OF THESE WERE THROWN INTO 1 MASS GRAVE.

NO ONE FOR SURE KNOWS HOW MANY GERMANS ESCAPED, PERHAPS AS MANY AS 50,000. THIS WOULD CAUSE BITTER DISPUTES BETWEEN THE AMERICANS AND BRITISH. HAD MONTGOMERY PUSHED HIS FORCES FAST ENOUGH? SHOULD BRADLEY HAVE DRAWN THE DIVISION LINE FARTHER UP? FOR NOW, IT DIDN'T MATTER. THOSE WHO HAD ESCAPED WOULD FIGHT AGAIN. THE GERMANS WERE RUNNING. THE AMERICANS AND BRITISH WERE PURSUING. EVERYONE WAS HEADED FOR PARIS.

NORMANDY

CHAPTER FIFTEEN

"AUX BARRICADES!"

HITLER'S PLAN TO DRIVE THE ALLIED INVASION BACK INTO THE SEA ENDED NOT ONLY IN FAILURE, IT ENDED IN DISASTER! 50,000 GERMAN SOLDIERS HAD BEEN KILLED OR HAD DIED OF WOUNDS SINCE D-DAY. 200,000 HAD BEEN CAPTURED. THE AMOUNT OF SUPPLIES AND EQUIPMENT LOST WAS STAGGERING, INCLUDING 1,300 TANKS.

STILL, 300,000 GERMANS SOLDIERS WOULD MAKE IT ACROSS THE SEINE AND, MORE REMARKABLY, 25,000 VEHICLES.

IN PARIS ON THE THE MORNING OF AUGUST 19, THE CITY'S GENDARMES TOOK POSSESSION OF THE PREFECTURE OF POLICE "IN THE NAME OF THE REPUBLIC AND CHARLES DE GAULLE."

WITHIN HOURS, THE COMMUNIST RESISTANCE UNDER THE COMMAND OF COLONEL ROL (AN ALIAS FOR HENRI TANGUY) JOINED IN BY AMBUSHING GERMAN SOLDIERS ALL OVER THE CITY. THEY WERE DISAPPOINTED THAT DE GAULLE'S PEOPLE HAD BEAT THEM TO THE PUNCH. ALL OVER THE CITY PEOPLE JOINED IN THE REBELLION, NO MATTER THEIR POLITICS.

THE VIOLENCE THAT SWEPT THROUGH THE STREETS WAS LIKE NOTHING THE CITY HAD EXPERIENCED IN OVER 4 YEARS OF OCCUPATION.

THE NEW GERMAN COMMANDER OF THE PARIS GARRISON WAS GEN. DIETRICH VON CHOLTITZ. HE HAD BEEN IN COMMAND FOR ONLY A FEW WEEKS AND WAS INSTRUCTED PERSONALLY BY HITLER TO DESTROY PARIS RATHER THAN LET IT FALL INTO ALLIED HANDS.

HE WAS A SOLDIER WHO ALWAYS FOLLOWED ORDERS. STILL, HE DIDN'T WANT TO BE KNOWN AS THE MAN WHO DESTROYED ONE OF THE WORLD'S MOST BEAUTIFUL CITIES. HE CONTACTED THE SWEDISH DIPLOMAT, RAOUL NORDLING.

USING NORDLING'S CONTACTS, VON CHOLTITZ "ALLOWED" A REPRESENTATIVE OF THE RESISTANCE TO CROSS ALLIED LINES. NORDLING AND VON CHOLTITZ BOTH KNEW THAT THE ONLY MAN WHO COULD SAVE PARIS WAS GEN. CHARLES DE GAULLE.

WHILE THE MESSENGER WAS ON HIS WAY TO MEET WITH THE ALLIED COMMANDER, VON CHOLTITZ TRIED TO ARRANGE A TRUCE WITH THE RESISTANCE. IT HELD FOR A SHORT TIME, BUT THE COMMUNIST RESISTANCE QUICKLY BROKE IT AND THE FIGHTING CONTINUED. COLONEL ROL WANTED TO GAIN CONTROL OF THE CITY BEFORE DE GAULLE ARRIVED, EVEN IF IT DESTROYED THE CITY AND "COST 200,000 LIVES."

THE POPULACE WAS RISING TO GREATER ACTION. THE CRY "AUX BARRICADES!" WAS HEARD EVERYWHERE. PEOPLE TORE UP COBBLESTONES AND TURNED OVER WAGONS AND CARS TO BUILD BARRICADES. IN 2 DAYS, 400 BARRICADES WERE BUILT, HAMPERING GERMAN MOVEMENT.

WHEN THE RESISTANCE REPRESENTATIVE REACHED ALLIED LINES, THE COMMANDERS WERE LESS THAN HAPPY TO SEE HIM. THEIR PLAN HAD BEEN TO BYPASS PARIS AND TAKE THE CITY IN SEPTEMBER WHEN THEY WOULD BE IN A BETTER POSITION TO FEED THE POPULATION.

HOWEVER, THEY QUICKLY MADE A DECISION. THE WORD WENT OUT TO CONTACT GENERAL LECLERC.

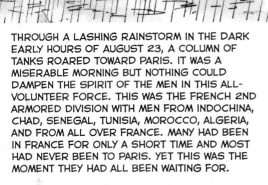

THROUGH A LASHING RAINSTORM IN THE DARK EARLY HOURS OF AUGUST 23, A COLUMN OF TANKS ROARED TOWARD PARIS. IT WAS A MISERABLE MORNING BUT NOTHING COULD DAMPEN THE SPIRIT OF THE MEN IN THIS ALL-VOLUNTEER FORCE. THIS WAS THE FRENCH 2ND ARMORED DIVISION WITH MEN FROM INDOCHINA, CHAD, SENEGAL, TUNISIA, MOROCCO, ALGERIA, AND FROM ALL OVER FRANCE. MANY HAD BEEN IN FRANCE FOR ONLY A SHORT TIME AND MOST HAD NEVER BEEN TO PARIS. YET THIS WAS THE MOMENT THEY HAD ALL BEEN WAITING FOR.

THEIR COMMANDER WAS A TALL, DISTINGUISHED ARISTOCRAT, THE VICOMTE JACQUES-PHILIPPE DE HAUTECLOCQUE. TO PROTECT HIS WIFE AND 6 CHILDREN WHO STILL LIVED IN FRANCE, HE HAD TAKEN THE NAME JACQUES LECLERC.

IT WAS MORE THAN 100 MILES TO PARIS, SO THEY DROVE QUICKLY DOWN THE NARROW DIRT COUNTRY ROAD AT TOP SPEED. OMAR BRADLEY DECIDED TO GIVE THEM A LITTLE HELP IN THE FORM OF THE U.S. 4TH INFANTRY DIVISION, WHICH HAD LANDED ON UTAH BEACH ON D-DAY.

VON CHOLTITZ HAD ALLOWED THE RESISTANCE TO CONTACT THE ALLIES, BUT HE WASN'T GOING TO GIVE UP PARIS WITHOUT A FIGHT. ON AUGUST 24, THE FRENCH 2ND ARMORED DIVISION RAN INTO A BAND OF 200 GERMAN 88MM GUNS.

AT GREAT COST, THE ALLIES FOUGHT THEIR WAY THROUGH THE DEFENSES. BY THAT EVENING THEY REACHED THE OUTSKIRTS OF PARIS. THE BELLS OF THE CITY RANG, ANNOUNCING THEIR ARRIVAL.

OTHERS ANNOUNCED THEIR ARRIVAL IN A BETTER WAY. THEY TELEPHONED THEIR PARENTS, FIANCÉES, AND CHILDREN.

AT DAWN THE NEXT MORNING, AUGUST 25, 1944, THE ADVANCE CONTINUED. TRAGICALLY, SEVERAL OF THOSE WHO HAD CALLED AHEAD WERE KILLED BEFORE THEY COULD MAKE THEIR PLANNED RENDEZVOUS. ONE FRENCHMAN WAS KILLED WITHIN VIEW OF THE CHURCH IN WHICH HE WAS MARRIED.

AS THE MORNING WORE ON, THE FRENCH 2ND ARMORED DIVISION, WITH THE U.S. 4TH BEHIND THEM, ENTERED THE CITY. THEY WERE STILL FIGHTING, BUT THEIR ARRIVAL SET OFF ONE OF THE MOST TUMULTOUS CELEBRATIONS OF ALL TIME. LONG HIDDEN TRI-COLORS FLUTTERED FROM WINDOWS ALONG WITH HOMEMADE VERSIONS OF THE STARS-AND-STRIPES.

THE PARISIANS SHOWERED THE DIRTY, WEARY SOLDIERS WITH FLOWERS AND CHAMPAGNE. THEY SMOTHERED THEM WITH KISSES AND HUGS. THE CRIES OF "VIVE DE GAULLE!", "VIVE LECLERC!", AND "MERCI! MERCI! MERCI!" FILLED THE AIR.

THE CITY WAS EXPLODING WITH JOY. ONE AMERICAN CAPTAIN SAID, "IT WAS LIKE A PHYSICAL WAVE OF HUMAN EMOTION PICKED US UP AND CARRIED US INTO THE HEART OF PARIS. IT WAS LIKE GROPING THROUGH A DREAM."

AT 1600, GENERAL DE GAULLE ARRIVED. THERE WAS LITTLE DOUBT THAT THIS TALL FIGURE, WHOM MOST PARISIANS HAD NEVER SEEN, WAS THE MAN OF THE HOUR THROUGH THE INCREDIBLE FORCE OF HIS WILL AND PERSONALITY. HE WAS A KING UNCROWNED.

THE AMERICAN G.I.S, DRUNK WITH VICTORY AND CHAMPAGNE, MARCHED ON THROUGH PARIS TOWARD GERMANY TO THE EAST. MANY, MANY OF THEIR COMRADES HAD BEEN LEFT BEHIND THEM IN THE FIELDS AND HEDGEROWS OF NORMANDY. THEY FELT GRAND TODAY BUT VERY TIRED. THERE WOULD BE NO REST FOR THEM...

...THE WAR WASN'T
OVER BY A LONG SHOT...

About the Author

Writer and artist Wayne Vansant was the primary artist for
Marvel's *The 'Nam* for more than five years. Since then he has
written and/or illustrated many historically accurate graphic histories
including *Antietam: The Fiery Trial* (for the National Park Service)
and *The Vietnam War: A Graphic History*. He is currently working
on *Gettysburg*, a graphic history of the Civil War's most famous battle.